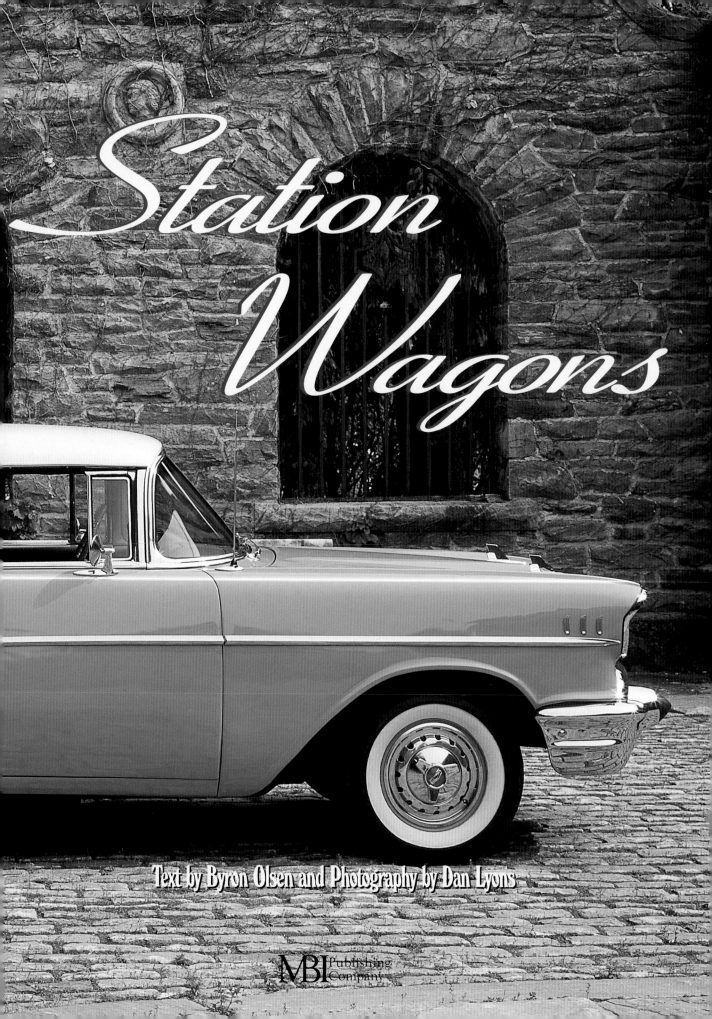

Station Wagons

Text by Byron Olsen and Photography by Dan Lyons

MBI Publishing Company

First published in 2000 by MBI Publishing Company, 729 Prospect Avenue, PO Box 1, Osceola, WI 54020-0001 USA

MBI Publishing Company books are also available at discounts in bulk quantity for industrial or sales-promotional use. For details write to Special Sales Manager at Motorbooks International Wholesalers & Distributors, 729 Prospect Avenue, PO Box 1, Osceola, WI 54020-0001 USA.

Library of Congress Cataloging-in-Publication Data

Olsen, Byron.
      Station wagons / Byron Olsen and Dan Lyons.
            p. cm.
      Includes index.
      ISBN 0-7603-0632-X (pbk. : alk. paper)
      1. Station wagons—United States—History.
      2. Woodies (Automobiles)—History. I. Lyons, Dan, II. Title.
   TL230.O437 2000   2000
   629.222—dc21
99-086227

On the front cover: Nearly every American automobile company produced and advertised a station wagon at some point in time. This collage depicts station wagon models found in Ford, Pontiac, Buick, and Packard sales catalogs from the 1930s through the 1950s. *Byron Olsen Collection*

On the frontispiece: Fins, that wonderful 1950s styling fad, were found on cars, trucks, and even station wagons. This 1956 Plymouth Sport Suburban, owned by Glenn and Barbara Patch, showcases Plymouth's first use of fins.

On the title page: The classic Chevrolet Nomad, built between 1955 and 1957, was so beautifully styled that one is hard pressed to think of it as a station wagon. This gorgeous 1957 Nomad belongs to Dave and Rosie Doran.

On the back cover: A trio of station wagons manufactured during the golden era. From the top are a 1959 Rambler Cross Country, owned by Bill Hicks, a 1962 Chevrolet Corvair Monza, owned by Wilbur Groesbeck, and a 1958 Buick Caballero, owned by Robert T. McIntyre.

Edited by Keith Mathiowetz

Text Design by Bruce Leckie

Cover Design by Dan Perry and Tom Heffron

Printed in Hong Kong

CONTENTS

PREFACE AND ACKNOWLEDGMENTS

This book is about North American–designed and –built station wagons. Reference sources concentrating on station wagons are scarce. Few books have been written on the subject, and those that have been tend to focus on the "woodies" of the 1930s and 1940s, which have become a collectible cult object today. David Fetherston has produced two interesting and useful books, one called *Woodys* and the other *American Woodys.* The latter book goes into some detail on Ford's wagon production facilities at Iron Mountain, Michigan, and also the development of the interesting Monart wagons at the beginning of World War II. I would like to particularly thank the author for the latter coverage.

Another book with good woody photos is *Classic Cars: Woodies, A National Treasure* by Bill Yenne.

Krause Publications has produced several publications that I have relied on extensively for reference. The most important are its *Standard Catalog* series. Time and again the *Standard Catalog* resolved questions of specifications, introduction and discontinuance dates, dimensions, and a whole host of other information needed to bring accuracy to the pages that follow. *Old Cars Weekly* newspaper, a Krause publication, frequently presents interesting articles on this or that aspect of station wagon history. Krause has also published a book by Ron Kowalke titled *Station Wagon, A Tribute to America's Workaholic on Wheels,* a collection of anecdotes and station wagon stories.

Another important reference to historians of the station wagon is the Crestline book Great *American Woodies and Wagons* by Donald Narus. Here in one concentrated chronological presentation are the basic elements of station wagon history. Narus has also written a fascinating book on the history of the Chrysler Town and Country wood-bodied cars.

Because there is so little on the bookshelf about wagons, the role played by periodicals became much more important. The key magazines I reference whenever I do automotive research are *Special Interest Autos* magazine, published by Hemmings Motor News, and *Collectible Automobile* magazine, published by Publications International, Ltd. These two magazines have consistently researched many aspects of the history of the automotive industry with both depth and accuracy. Both of these magazines also have done a superb job of interviewing designers and engineers from the automotive industry and making a permanent record of their recollections. To an automotive historian, the word

"invaluable" is not nearly strong enough. My thanks to these publications in particular.

Other reference sources include *Motor Trend* magazine issues from the 1950s (I never throw anything away relating to automobile history), *Automobile Quarterly* magazine, and *Consumer Reports.* Wagons were a practical car and thus got a lot of attention from *Consumer Report.*

Station wagons, for some reason, have not caught on with very many car collectors as yet. As a result, it was difficult to find preserved, show-quality wagons to be photographed for this book. All of the contemporary views of station wagons in this book were photographed by Dan Lyons, who worked very hard to locate and photograph interesting and significant station wagons for this book. Thank you, Dan, for your superb-quality work.

Ultimately, the most comprehensive source of both station wagon information and station wagon pictures proved to be my own extensive collection of automobile sales literature. Since 1946, I've been making the rounds of car dealers for every make every year and have carefully saved all of the catalogs and folders that I picked up. These sales materials have always fascinated me because they show the cars as the manufacturers and creators wanted them to appear. Often these renditions made the wagons appear longer and lower than they really were, and probably reflected the way the manufacturers wished they looked. The sales catalogs also answered many questions about specifications and variations unique to the station wagon body style.

Helping me get all this on paper with accuracy, and expertise, not to mention infinite patience, is my friend, Debi Prozinski, who has performed similar service for me in the past. Thank you, Debi. Thanks also to my good car friends and fellow members of various car clubs who were often good for confirming bits of needed information.

Finally, I would like to thank my editor, Keith Mathiowetz, for his help throughout, especially with picture selection. I hope this book contributes to developing more interest among car collectors in saving and restoring station wagons. Wagons are more interesting than sedans and certainly have a lot more versatility, which can be as much fun to a collector as it was to the original buyer.

—*Byron Olsen*
St. Paul, Minnesota
December 1999

INTRODUCTION

The station wagon was a uniquely American automotive design development. From the early days of the twentieth century, which coincided with the dawn of the age of the automobile, the wagon idea took hold in North America. That idea sought more room for passengers and luggage than could be found in a standard automobile. Early primitive examples of the station wagon concept were usually built more like trucks and buses than cars. That's where the history of the American station wagon began to diverge from the rest of the world. The American wagon became definitely a car-based vehicle. Elsewhere in the world, higher-capacity vehicles developed as utilitarian vans and small buses. Only in the years following World War II did world auto manufacturers begin to develop cars with greater capacity as well. While these design efforts usually followed the American idea of a squared-off body with a tailgate and removable seats, they were almost always utilitarian, Spartan vehicles at the bottom of the glamour ladder.

Not in the United States, however. The American station wagon soon developed into a style statement overshadowing its utilitarian purpose. By the 1940s, station wagons were becoming expensive glamour cars and less and less practical.

The story of the American station wagon tracks the evolution of the American automobile. From a utilitarian truck-like vehicle, to a car-based vehicle, to a style statement, and finally to a universal family vehicle is the storyline of the American station wagon. Along the way, the station wagon got involved in every fad and trend that other American cars displayed: increased power and luxury; longer and lower designs; tailfins; glamorous hardtop body configurations; and, finally, downsizing and economy after the energy crisis of the 1970s. Truly, the history of American station wagons keeps step with the development of the American automobile.

Like the automobile, the history of the station wagon also spans the twentieth century. Unfortunately, the end of the century has almost brought us to the end of the station wagon, at least as built on American car chassis. As the millennium closed, there remained but a handful of American-built station wagons, if truck-based and sport utility vehicles were not counted.

The golden age of the station wagon in terms of volume production was the 1960s. I came of age as the station wagon boom was escalating and raised my family during the years the boom was at its height. My wife and I always bought station wagons in those child-rearing years and she still drives a minivan today. We thought the station wagon with its folding rear seat was the greatest idea since sliced bread. Throw an air mattress in the back and it became a mobile playpen where kids could romp around, play with toys, sleep, or whatever. No longer were small children doomed to sit confined in a cramped back seat and suffer through the eternal boredom of a motor trip.

That's all gone now. Modern safety concerns won't let us leave children or even adults unrestrained inside a moving motor vehicle. That's as it should be and the declining death and injury rate from automotive travel reflects the wisdom of those decisions. Minivans, vans, and trucks offer greater cargo capacity than even the biggest station wagon. In a sense, vehicles have become more specialized and the all-purpose station wagon has lost out. But I confess to a certain nostalgia for the sight of a grand, yacht-like Ford Country Squire or Chrysler Town and Country festooned with faux woodwork charging down the interstate with the roof rack piled high and the interior filled with a family heading off on a grand tour of America.

Enjoy this swing down a highway of history as we explore all the fascinating details of station wagon history and development. It's all here: from woodies, to hardtops, to econoboxes, and minivans.

Here it is, the grandaddy of all station wagons, the 1929 Ford Model A. This splendid example shows us the characteristics that set the pattern for station wagons for years to come. The structural framing of the body, using a darker-colored wood, is on the outside of the body panels. There are four doors and the whole rig is built on a passenger car chassis.

CHAPTER 1
– The 1920s –

THE ORIGIN OF THE SPECIES

The history of the station wagon body type is almost as old as the automobile industry. The saga of the station wagon that we'll look at in this book starts after World War I in the roaring 1920s. The motor car was coming of age and the decade of the 1920s saw cars become reliable and car ownership become widespread. In 1920, cars were toys for the rich: by 1929, cars had become a necessity for many. The automobile was on the verge of becoming the centerpiece of modern society.

The station wagon came by its name honestly. Until automobile ownership became widespread, the only way to travel between cities was by passenger train. There were no airlines and very few airplanes, and there was no network of paved highways to permit one to drive from city to city. So when people traveled for business or pleasure, they took the train. When they arrived at their destination city, the railroad deposited them at the local railroad station. This was usually downtown, but not always. In larger cities there were cabs. Livery stables, where one could rent a horse, were common before the 1920s, but rental car agencies as a replacement did not become common until much later.

Taxicabs were for the well-heeled, and the average American traveler couldn't afford to use them. That left the typical traveler, laden with luggage, with the alternative of walking or taking the streetcar, if there was one. And that was assuming the traveler knew where he/she was going in a strange city.

Another view of the car that set the pattern for the station wagon: the 1929 Ford Model A. Shown here is a rear view, with the car rigged for foul weather with side curtains in place. It would be 10 years before the canvas side curtains on these early models would be replaced with windows.

Enter the station wagon. These were vehicles sent by hotels to meet the train and ferry passengers and potential hotel guests back to the hotel: A wagon that went to the station. Some hotels used standard touring cars, but that limited seating to three or four people and not much luggage. This gave rise to a new cottage industry: wagon builders who took a truck or large-car chassis and constructed simple wooden bodies with more seats than the car body.

At the beginning of the 1920s, there was little distinction between automobiles and trucks. Consequently, any large automobile chassis would do. A wooden body was easy to build with several bench seats, flat roof, and open sides. It was a truck bed with seats and a roof, leaving room in the back for luggage.

Early station wagon bodies were very squared off with simple lines, much like the vehicles upon which they were mounted. Wood was easy to work with in fabricating bodies. There was not a large demand for these bodies, thus setting up a production operation to stamp out metal bodies was prohibitively expensive. These early wagon bodies could be built one at a time in a small shop.

Thus was born the station wagon: the wagon that went down to the station to meet all the trains and deliver people to the more popular destinations in that city or town.

By the mid-1920s, a wagon-building industry had started to develop. Several body builders who eventually built station wagon

All set for a picnic in our 1929 Ford Model A. The picnic kit and the oilcloth table mat were essential ingredients for picnics at the time.

bodies in the 1930s and 1940s for Detroit automobile manufacturers got their start at this time. Some of the names that survived to the 1940s included Cantrell, York, Ionia, Seaman, and Hercules. These early bodies were usually built on larger truck chassis rather than car chassis. There was little weather protection provided. There was a windshield and a roof to keep the rain off, but seldom any side windows, although roll-down canvas side curtains were often supplied.

The wagon builders began to advertise their wares for other uses. Ads even found their way into upper-crust magazines such as *Country Life*. You could pick up a station wagon for motoring around your estate.

These hybrid vehicles were often referred to as "depot hacks." Hack was a slang word for taxi, and depot, of course, referred to the railroad station.

Certain features of station wagon architecture were established during the 1920s, and

became more or less standard design features of automobile-based wagons of the 1930s and 1940s. These wagons usually had more than two seats, three being a common number. The sides and doors were made up of wood panels with the structural framework of the door or the side panel on the outside, displayed against the backdrop of the filler panel. In other words, the structural members were outside the body. The wood sides and posts were usually varnished rather than painted and the framework pieces were often varnished in a color different from the paneling. This use of two types of wood finished in contrasting colors continued to the end of wood-bodied wagons and even continued on modern station wagons garnished with imitation woodwork.

The impetus, then, for the station wagon was to get a cheap, readily available vehicle equipped to carry extra people and provide some additional room for luggage and other gear. The distances traveled were short, so windows and

side weather protection were not considered to be worth the expense and effort. Glass side windows in station wagons did not become common until the late 1930s.

Another virtue of these early station wagons was their ability to survive in rough road conditions that would be too hard on a regular automobile. They were rugged, simple, even primitive vehicles.

An important event that changed the future of the station wagon occurred in 1929. Ford Motor Company decided to manufacture its own station wagon bodies and converted a plant it owned in Iron Mountain, Michigan, for the purpose. Henry Ford was then a big fan of vertical integration of his industrial empire. He not only wanted to own the plants that manufactured the finished product, the automobile, he wanted to own all of the sources of supply. Ford Motor Company eventually even made its own steel and glass. In the case of the station wagon, this led Ford to not only set up its own plant in upper Michigan to build bodies, but also to own the forests where the wood was grown.

The plant in Iron Mountain had actually been built in 1920 to make wooden parts for the Model T. By 1929, Ford had converted production to the Model A, which used very little wood by comparison with other cars of the day. Ford no longer needed the production capacity to make a lot of wood parts for the basic automobiles.

Station wagon bodies had become common additions to Ford Model Ts. By building its own station wagon bodies, Ford could expand the market for its automobiles and capture the revenue for itself. At the same time, it could make use of a factory that had become surplus.

Thus, in 1929, Ford added a station wagon to its line of automobiles and began to advertise it. This marks the first time an automobile manufacturer offered a station wagon as part of its regular catalog of body types. Initially, Ford listed the station wagon only in the truck catalog, even though it was built on the car chassis. The 1929 Ford station wagon had four doors and was built on the Model A car chassis. Although the roof had a slope down to the windshield, that was the only curve on the entire wooden body. Someone familiar with wagons of the 1940s would recognize the decorative framing on the sides of this wagon and tailgate. But there was no glass in the windows anywhere along the side or the rear.

Nevertheless, the new body type was popular. In spite of selling for a whopping $695, Ford produced 5,200 for the 1929 model year.

Although Ford built the wagon parts at its Iron Mountain, Michigan, plant, these components were then shipped to the Murray Body Company of Detroit or the Beeker-Rawling Company in Cleveland to be assembled into wagon bodies. With this boost by one of the largest automobile manufacturers, the station wagon was now poised for new markets and new growth.

By the end of the 1920s, closed automobiles had replaced open touring cars as the most common automotive body type. Station wagons built for the purpose could accommodate more people and carry more baggage than sedans. The 1930s would see more and more car manufacturers develop that wagon-hauling advantage over sedans.

The rear compartment of the 1929 Ford Model A, the first production station wagon. The canvas side curtains are in place and the slatted wood roof construction can be clearly seen. The bucket seats are a sporty touch.

A 1935 Ford station wagon. This was a good sales year for Ford, as it outsold rival Chevrolet. The wagon body style was now a well-established part of the Ford line, but archrival Chevrolet would not catalog a wagon for four more years. *Byron Olsen*

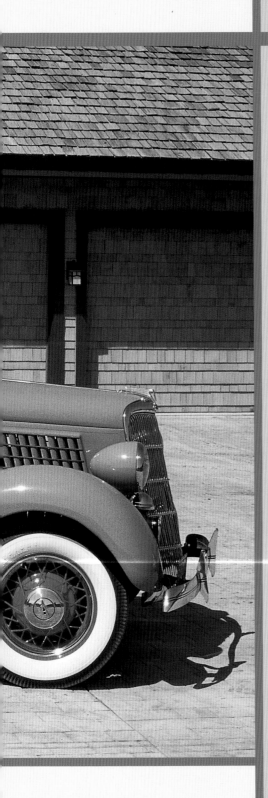

CHAPTER 2
– The 1930s –

THE DEPRESSION AND SWIFT EVOLUTION IN THE AUTOMOTIVE INDUSTRY

In spite of Ford introducing a station wagon body type into its regular lineup of passenger car offerings, other manufacturers did not rush to follow Ford's lead. The best explanation is probably the onset of the Great Depression triggered by the stock market crash in the fall of 1929. The bad news was sinking in fast as 1930 began and sales of all types of automobiles began to suffer almost immediately. Although several manufacturers turned out station wagons built by the various wagon body builders, most were on a custom-order basis.

By 1931, even Ford could only manage to build 3,000 station wagons. By the end of the year Ford discontinued production of station wagon parts at its Iron Mountain plant and once again began buying wood wagon parts from outside suppliers. But Ford did continue to catalog a station wagon in its lineup of available models. Wagon sales were dropping, but Ford kept the station wagon alive.

The Depression began to bottom out by 1933. Dodge and Plymouth contracted with U.S. Body and Forging Company to build wagon bodies for the two companies. Dodge named its design the Westchester Semi-Sedan. It was, of course, constructed of wood, but cars and trucks were now starting to become a bit curvy and streamlined. The Dodge Westchester adopted a first for the station wagon body design: roll-up front door windows in place of side curtains. The roof was curved transversely as well

The front compartment of a 1935 Ford station wagon. "Functional" and "utilitarian" were the key words. *Byron Olsen*

as longitudinally. This design shed water better and looked more stylish.

Dodge, Plymouth, and Ford were the only automobile manufacturers cataloging station wagons at this point. All three considered them trucks even though some were built on passenger car chassis. Tailgates were of the drop-down variety. There was no upper liftgate: just a roll-up or removable curtain.

The economy had improved to the point in 1935 that Ford reopened its station wagon body parts plant at Iron Mountain, Michigan. The Ford wagon bodies were again assembled by Murray Body Company in Detroit using parts supplied by Ford. The Ford automobile design was changed rather significantly for 1935, necessitating a change in the lines of the wagon bodies. Ford wagons now also offered wind-up front door windows. The Ford catalog text shows that the appeal of the station wagon body design was becoming evident. It stated: "It combines the facilities of a passenger car and a light haul-

ing unit. It carries seven passengers comfortably. The rear seats are quickly and easily removed providing space for carrying baggage."

The year 1935 saw what turned out to be a significant event in station wagon history. The Chevrolet CarryAll was introduced, which soon became known as the Suburban. The CarryAll had windows all around, two upholstered removable bench seats, in addition to the front seats, and room for eight passengers. This was a truck-based vehicle rather than being built on a car chassis. It certainly lays claim to being the first all-steel station wagon, although some would argue that it was built as a commercial vehicle on a truck chassis rather than an automobile for recreational and pleasure use. In fact, it was made by punching windows in the sides of the panel truck body. This original Chevy Suburban offered only the two doors of the panel truck from which it was made. Several decades would pass before these vehicles would offer more than two doors. The first all-steel car-sized wagon was the 1946 Willys Jeep station wagon.

Eyeing a good thing, additional car manufacturers entered the wagon marketplace in 1936. Oldsmobile and Hudson showed (but did not catalog) wagons that year, and the next year, 1937, witnessed some Packard and Studebaker wagons. Ford began assembling its own wagon bodies at the Iron Mountain plant. This was another first. Glass windows were slowly making their way around the entire wagon body, although sometimes as an option. Pontiac and DeSoto also exhibited wagons in 1937.

The station wagon was beginning to make a fashion statement. The arrangement of the exterior vertical and horizontal braces varied from body builder to body builder more as a style distinction than a structural necessity. Different kinds of wood were used and stained different colors for style. U.S.

Body & Forge Company, one of the body builders used by Plymouth and Dodge, used a distinctive red gum wood for the belt-molding strip. Curves began to appear in station wagon architecture. There was seldom any curvature to the sides of the body or the tailgate area as yet, but the roof sloped up from the sedan windshield to the rear of the body and usually showed some curvature.

The American automobile underwent a styling transition in 1939. It was the year that headlight placement migrated from a position on the side of the hood just back of the grill to a new location down on the fenders. Mating the ever-more-rounded sheet metal of the passenger car front ends with square wagon bodies presented greater challenges to the station wagon body builders who had largely limited themselves to straight lines in the wagon bodies. The shape of car design by the end of the 1930s evolved into round, streamlined, and in many cases,

The cargo end of a 1935 Ford wagon. With the third seat in place, there's not much room for luggage unless it's parked on the tailgate. There's no upper tailgate as this wagon still uses side curtains for weather protection.
Byron Olsen

The 1938 Pontiac station wagon as presented in the Pontiac sales catalog. Judging by the well-dressed couple and the even better-dressed person handling the luggage, Pontiac was not aiming at the truck market. This is one of the few wagons to appear in a car sales catalog during the 1930s. *Byron Olsen Collection*

teardrop shapes. These shapes did not lend themselves to accommodating extra passengers or large amounts of gear in sedan form. This may have contributed to the growth of station wagon sales.

Chevrolet cataloged a station wagon built of wood and built on a passenger car chassis for the first time in 1939. Ionia was the body builder and continued to supply wood wagons for General Motors cars right up to the last one offered, the 1953 Buick.

The decade of the 1930s saw the wagon make the transition from a crude truck to a cataloged body style in several passenger car manufacturers' lines. The wagon had made its place in the automotive sunshine. The best was about to come in the 1940s.

A passenger car–based station wagon design had evolved. As closed passenger car bodies limited the number of people that could be carried, the wagon developed as a vehicle in which more passengers could be carried at something close to passenger car

comfort, but at the same time have a greater capacity for luggage and other cargo. Sedans of the 1930s had small luggage compartments or none at all, perhaps giving a bit of an impetus to early wagon development. Wagons built on car chassis used a square wooden body, a front seat, a back seat and, usually, a third seat behind the rear axle. The shape in the back was that of a box, while in front the sedan windshield was usually retained, cut off at the header. Many 1930s wagons did not have glass in the side windows and rear window, or used glass only in the front door windows. Instead, side curtains were used just as in early open touring cars. By the end of the decade, however, almost all wagons had adopted side windows made of glass instead of side curtains.

As we have seen, Ford, by the mid-1930s, set up its own mill and factory on Michigan's Upper Peninsula to manufacture its own wagon bodies. Other wagon body builders started in Michigan because of the

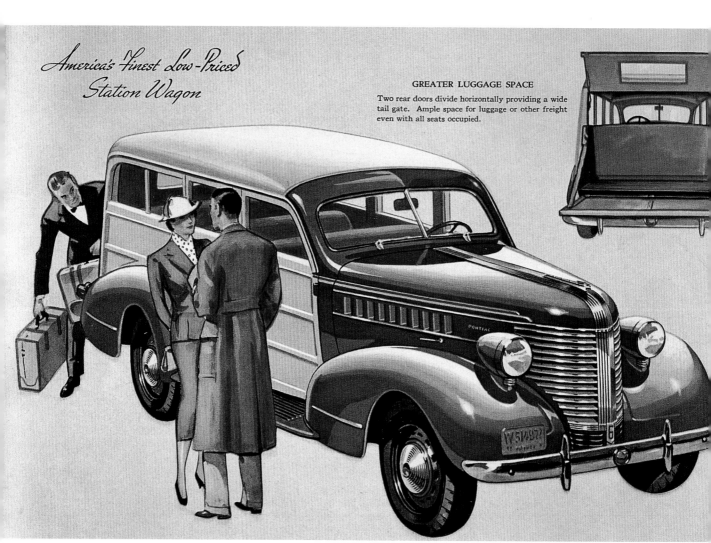

America's Finest Low-Priced Station Wagon

GREATER LUGGAGE SPACE

Two rear doors divide horizontally providing a wide tail gate. Ample space for luggage or other freight even with all seats occupied.

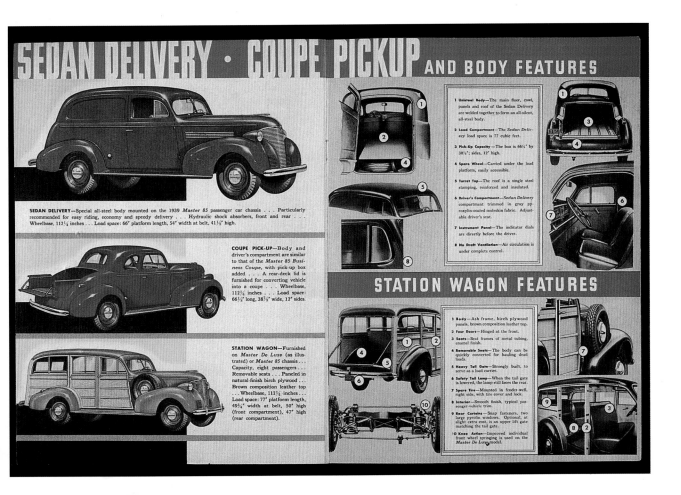

proximity to the automobile factories in southern Michigan and the hardwood forests of the upper peninsula. This is where Ionia and others were located.

On a separate front, the design of the original "depot hack" station wagon was diverging from what we have come to know as the station wagon. High-capacity commercial station wagons evolved on a different path from the car-based wagons. Led by the Chevrolet CarryAll Suburban, light truck chassis were used and several manufacturers produced wood-bodied station wagons with more seating capacity than car-based wagons. Wood was used for the same reasons, i.e., it was easy and cheap to fabricate on a low-production custom basis. Eventually these working vehicles adopted steel construction and evolved into the vans and small buses seen today in airport, hotel, and hospital service.

Wood had been used all along for economy. It was easy to work with and it was cheap. These virtues were desirable because wagons were low-production, low-selling vehicles. It was much cheaper to make them out of wood, almost by hand in some cases,

than it was to tool up jigs and presses to stamp them out of steel.

Here's a chart showing the growth in the number of wagons offered as more or less regular-production body types by U.S. car companies during the 1930s. Not all of these wagons appear in the sales catalogs, but could be ordered by dealers. Some other manufacturers produced station wagons on a special-order basis. A few manufacturers who were selling to several different automobile builders were supplying most of the wagon bodies by this time. This listing should be taken with a grain of salt because it is difficult to confirm the production status for some of these marques. However, there is photographic evidence that at least one example of every marque and year listed was built.

This table illustrates that wagons were finding a regular place in the automobile production lineup. In 1938, Ford produced 6,000 station wagons for the calendar year. Dodge built 375 units and Plymouth 555 units the same year. This was sufficient enough sales to make more and more other manufacturers take notice and consider adding station wagons to their car lines.

The first year Chevrolet cataloged a station wagon on the passenger car chassis was in 1939. However, it was only listed in the truck catalog. The Master Deluxe shown here used independent front suspension and seated eight passengers. The wagon was also available on the Master Eighty-Five chassis with solid front axle. Seen here are some other car-based utility models popular at the time. *Byron Olsen Collection*

THE NEW "*Westchester*"*

• THE 1936 PLYMOUTH with "Westchester" semi-sedan sub-urban body . . . the last word in utility and reliability, with Plymouth economy and genuine Hydraulic Brakes. Full glass enclosed . . . equipped with safety glass and window-lift controls—or curtains. Rattle-proof seats for 7 to 8 pas-sengers, on the best engineered chassis in the low-price field. Ask any Dodge, De Soto or Chrysler dealer for details.

By PLYMOUTH

* "Westchester" - Trade Mark Registered U. S. Pat. Off. by U. S. Body and Forging Co., Inc.

YEAR	CAR-BASED	TRUCK-BASED
1930	Ford	
1931	Ford	
1932	Ford	
1933	Ford, Plymouth	Dodge
1934	Ford, Plymouth	Dodge
1935	Ford, Plymouth	Chevrolet, Dodge, International
1936	Ford, Dodge, Plymouth, Hudson, Olds	Chevrolet, International, Ford
1937	Pontiac, Hudson, Studebaker, DeSoto, Ford, Plymouth, Packard, Dodge	Chevrolet, GMC, International, Ford
1938	Pontiac, Ford, Plymouth, Dodge, Hudson, Studebaker	Chevrolet, Ford, GMC, International
1939	Chevrolet, Ford, Plymouth, Willys, Hudson, Pontiac, Oldsmobile, Studebaker, Packard	Chevrolet, Ford, GMC, International

Chevrolet joined the ranks of builders of station wagons on car chassis in 1939. The same year, Plymouth became the second auto manufacturer to build and assemble its own station wagon bodies.

Thus, the 1930s proved to be a decade of significant change to the station wagon concept. Until Ford began building passenger car station wagons, the station wagon was strictly a utilitarian commercial vehicle and was more truck than car. It was built for the commercial purpose of hauling passengers. By the end of the decade, the station wagon as we know it today had evolved into an alternative body style available in many passenger car lines. No longer was its primary purpose commercial: station wagons fell into the pleasure car category and were even becoming stylish. The American wood station wagon was about to enter its golden age.

This 1936 Plymouth carries a body built by U.S. Body & Forging Co., Inc. and named "Westchester." It is a good example of the station wagon body design beginning to appear on passenger car chassis. Although not listed in the Plymouth sales catalog, this model had a folder of its own and was clearly being marketed by Chrysler Corporation dealers. *Byron Olsen Collection*

One of the most elegant wood-bodied wagons of the 1940s, and one of the most valuable today, is this 1941 Packard 120. Power is supplied by one of Packard's legendary 120-horsepower straight-eights. Spare tires were carried in side mounts in the front fenders, a lingering holdover from the luxury cars of the 1930s. It provided a convenient answer to the station wagon spare tire problem, but automotive styling trends soon eliminated this option.

CHAPTER 3
– The 1940s –

THE STATION WAGON IS ESTABLISHED AS AN AUTOMOBILE WITH STYLE

As the 1940s dawned, World War II was already under way in Europe. Although the United States would not enter the war until December of 1941, production of war materials was building up rapidly for shipment to Great Britain and other countries with which the United States would soon be allied. In large part because of the war-induced industrial production, prosperity was returning to America. People had more opportunities to travel and more spending money. Perhaps this was a factor that began to increase the popularity of the station wagon body style. A camping trip, a visit to the lake, or a vacation with a big family severely taxed the trunk capacity of sedans of the day. But a station wagon could accommodate lots of luggage and camping gear, as well as additional people.

Whatever the reason, by 1940, station wagons had become an established body type offered by most low- and medium-priced auto manufacturers. Ford remained the leader and indeed would lead in station wagon sales into the 1980s when the station wagon began to fade from popularity. Ford's competitors in the low-price field, Chevrolet and Plymouth, both offered station wagons by 1939. Thereafter, the wagon was a permanent addition to those car lineups.

Buick introduced its Estate Wagon in 1940, and from there to the end of wooden wagon production in 1953, built the most luxurious and expensive station wagon in the U.S. market, rivaled only by Packard in some years. Pontiac started building wagons in 1937 and would continue throughout the

A long and sleek 1942 Hudson Super 6. Hudson built its last station wagons in 1941 and 1942, and not many at that. Hudsons during these years held many speed records and so this was probably one of the faster wagons on the block. *John Conde Collection*

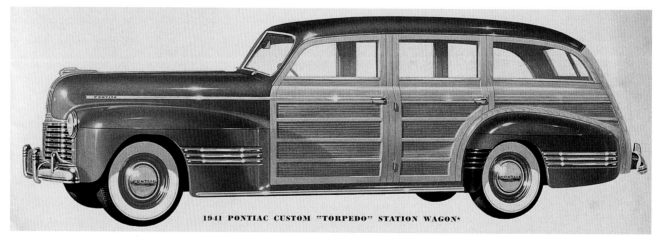

1941 PONTIAC CUSTOM "TORPEDO" STATION WAGON*

A 1941 Pontiac Custom "Torpedo" station wagon. This elegant wagon was available with six- or eight-cylinder engines and genuine leather upholstery with chrome-finished tubular seat frames throughout. Pontiacs carried a lot of chrome in those days, and the effect of the chrome ribs in the fenders was repeated by the extra horizontal ribs on the wagon doors. *Byron Olsen Collection*

wagon era. Oldsmobile built wagons through the decade of the 1940s and then ended wagon production in 1950. As the station wagon body style became widely popular in the 1950s, Oldsmobile returned to the wagon fold by 1957.

In the General Motors family, only Cadillac has never cataloged a station wagon. However, as a sure indication that station wagons had come to represent something that was a bit stylish, there were a number of custom-built Cadillac wagons constructed during the 1940s by the surviving coach builders of the classic era. After the market for custom-bodied luxury cars dried up in the 1930s, survivors such as Bohman and Schwartz, and Coachcraft turned to fancy station wagons to help keep their doors open. The desire of well-heeled buyers to own the top-of-the-line led to custom-built Cadillac station wagons being produced through the 1950s and even as late as the 1970s.

Plymouth built station wagons every year during the 1940s. Dodge built a few wagons in

A 1941 Chevrolet Special Deluxe station wagon. This was only the third year of Chevy wagon production, which probably explains why only 2,045 cars were built in 1941. All the usual wagon architecture of woodies of the 1940s is seen here: the fabric-covered roof, the all-wood construction with the framing in a contrasting color, and the tailgate-mounted spare tire with the bumper cut out so the tailgate can be opened with the spare in place.

The front compartment of a 1941 Chevrolet Special Deluxe station wagon. This is a typical wagon interior of the 1940s. Note the rubber floor mats with carpet inserts and the leather seat trim. The dashboard is woodgrained metal, but the door panel and window moldings are all real wood.

1938 but then built none until 1949. DeSoto also dabbled with a few special-order wagons in 1937 but did not offer a station wagon as a regular part of its lineup until 1949. Chrysler built the Town and Country in 1941 and 1942, one of the most unusual station wagons of the 1940s. Chrysler also built an interesting but wildly impractical series of wooden-bodied cars that were not station wagons at all, but were coupes, convertibles, and sedans. More about this shortly.

Among the independent manufacturers that survived the Depression, only Hudson, Packard, and Willys offered station wagons during the 1940s. Hudson built a few in 1941 and 1942 and then left the wagon market forever. Actually there is an exception to that statement, but a technical one. After Nash and Hudson merged to form American Motors in 1954, Nash Ramblers, including Rambler station wagons, were sold for two or three years with Hudson as well as Nash nameplates. So, technically we must concede that there were Hudson station wagons built after World War II.

Packard offered station wagons through 1941 on the 110 and 120 chassis (the 110 was a six-cylinder and the 120 was an eight). Then Packard dropped wagons until 1948 when it sold a few mostly steel-bodied wagons. These 1948 and 1949 Packard wagons were unusual but were actually the first large-size steel station wagons introduced in the United States. There was wood in the tailgate assembly and wood applied as an applique around the side windows. However, the roof and inner body structure were steel. The styling of the 1948 Packard adopted a full-fendered design where the front fender line flowed continuously through to the rear. This meant the doors were no longer exposed and were covered by the extended fender. There was no place to show woodwork below the beltline, so Packard cut panels out of the two doors and installed wood panels to keep the station wagon look. The side doors were otherwise interchangeable with Packard sedans. The effect was not altogether successful, as the wood door panels looked tacked-on as an afterthought.

Packard called their wagon a Station Sedan and advertised it as "the successor to the station wagon." The body contours tapered in at the rear. This gave a more streamlined appearance in contrast to the square boxlike shape of other station wagons at the time, although this shape reduced the Packard's cargo space. These were expensive cars and were not very popular. An estimated 3,864 were produced from 1947 through 1949.

Willys cataloged a station wagon in 1940 and 1941 in the Americar line. This was a compact car smaller than anything offered by major

This 1941 Packard interior view shows typical roof construction of an all-wood station wagon body. It also shows the great amount of costly cabinet-making work that went into a true woody.

U.S. manufacturers. It was powered by a four-cylinder engine, which became the basic power plant for the world-famous Jeep. After World War II, Willys did not resurrect the Americar but instead converted its entire production to Jeep-based vehicles.

The 1946 Willys all-steel station wagon was a true trailblazer. Unlike the truck-based Chevy and GMC Suburbans, the Willys Jeep was the first all-steel wagon designed and built to be a passenger car. There was no wood on the exterior although the sheet metal was stamped with ribs and depressed panels that looked a bit like wood

Another elegant Packard woody, a 1941 six-cylinder 110 model. This one shows all the characteristics of wood wagon architecture: light-colored framing with darker, probably mahogany, panels, and fabric-covered roof.

when painted contrasting tan and brown colors. That's just what Willys did for the first few years of production. The only wood pieces in the vehicle were some skid strips in the cargo area. The Willys Jeep wagon was designed by noted industrial designer Brooks Stevens of Milwaukee, Wisconsin. Stevens' name turns up several times in this history of station wagons because he produced two of the most significant designs in the history of the station wagon: the original 1946 Jeep wagon and the 1963 Jeep Wagoneer.

This Jeep wagon was nimble and easy to handle and could also carry a lot of stuff because of its boxy, squared-off body design. It was a trailblazer in another sense, also. By 1949, it became available with the trademark Jeep four-wheel-drive system and thus became the progenitor of today's legion of sport utility vehicles. This practical, sturdy wagon and the civilian version of the four-wheel-drive Jeep kept Willys reasonably healthy and growing modestly for the next several decades. The Jeep Wagoneer and Cherokee led the sport utility field in the 1980s and 1990s and eventually made Jeep the most valuable component of American Motors when Chrysler bought AMC in 1987.

By 1940, side curtains had been done away with and all station wagons used glass in the

The DeLuxe Plymouth station wagon in 1940, its second year as a cataloged model. The rear door windows and rear quarter windows slide open and the front door windows roll down. Plymouths, like all Chrysler products during these years, had progressive engineering and were very pleasant cars to drive. The lack of color contrast between the wood paneling and wood framing is unusual. *Byron Olsen Collection*

side windows, door windows, and tailgates. Several continued to use sliding glass rather than wind-down glass in the rear side doors. By the end of the decade, only Chrysler Corporation wagons were still using sliding windows in the rear side doors. The all-steel wagons Chrysler introduced in 1950 switched to roll-up windows. However, the Plymouth Suburban two-door wagons and indeed most two-door wagons built through the 1950s continued to use sliding side windows for the back seat.

Wagons might have been bigger sellers in the 1940s if they had been priced lower. However, wooden station wagons had become a premium, semi-hand-built, low-production product. They were usually priced at the top end of each car maker's line, so relatively few were sold.

Until the last years of the wood wagon era, the wood throughout the body was structural as well as ornamental. The framing was bolted and screwed together over the side panels and the tailgate, and the roof fabric was tacked on over the top crossbows. Roof construction consisted of closely spaced, latticelike cross strips or longitudinal strips curved to establish the roof contour. These wood strips were then covered with heavy oilcloth fabric or canvas. This construction method almost without exception continued until 1948. Up to that time, all wagons (with the exception of the Willys Jeep), were prewar designs

carried over and put back into production after World War II ended. The first new postwar wagons were introduced in 1948 and 1949. Without exception, all of these new wagons had steel roofs and steel inner structures even though there were varying amounts of wood still used in the side panels, doors, and tailgates.

Wooden wagons were high maintenance. This was another factor that restricted sales. The joints, bolts, and screws tended to loosen up after only a short while, giving rise to squeaks and rattles in the body. Most sedan bodies were all steel by this time and resisted the development of rattles much better than station wagons. In a serious collision, a station wagon could be reduced to kindling wood. The curved steel of the sedan resisted collision impact much better than the flat wooden panels of a wagon.

But the most notorious feature of wooden station wagons was the poor durability of the finish. A wagon literally had to be revarnished every year, or the wood would start to deteriorate. The fabric roof also required periodic coating and replacement. Many owners got fed up with this routine. This high maintenance held down sales and eventually led to the all-steel station wagon. As wagon popularity grew during the 1940s, it became clear that there would have to be a conversion to a more durable and less-expensive method of construction. Failure

The 1941 Ford Super DeLuxe station wagon. Ford was a consistent leader in station wagon sales and most were powered by Ford's famous flathead V-8. Although a new six-cylinder engine was introduced in 1941, it was not even mentioned in the sales catalog. *Byron Olsen Collection*

to refinish the bodies frequently led to a high mortality rate. Wood rot developing in the body structure led to a premature grave for many wagons. This fragility plus low sales initially explains why surviving wood wagons are so rare and valued today.

There was another factor pushing the industry toward steel wagons. Independent firms, which supplied the bodies on order to the car manufacturers, built most wagon bodies. The method of fabrication was very labor intensive and costly. This almost-hand-built production would not permit volume sales or lower prices.

Thus, the 1940s saw the transition from wood construction to steel bodies. It happened rather swiftly. All of the new wagon designs introduced in 1948 and 1949 had steel roofs and steel inner structure. Wood continued to be used in varying degrees for decorative effect on the exterior and on the interior as well. The 1949 Ford wagons had wood panels set into the steel sides somewhat like the Packard. Ford offered only two-door wagons during the years 1949 through 1951. The Mercury used the same body as the Ford during this period. When introduced in 1949, the Ford wagon still had a wood-covered tailgate, but by the end of production in 1951, the tailgate and transom were all steel.

With the exception of Buick, all General Motors station wagons (Chevrolet, Pontiac, and Oldsmobile) introduced in 1949 were built with the same body. This new body used a steel roof and had flow-through fender lines that left little of the side of the body exposed. There was some wood around the windows and below the belt molding although it was laid-over steel and was not structural. The tailgate and transom still had lots of wood in them.

Clearly, the race to steel was on at General Motors because early in the 1949 production run, all three of these marques began offering all-steel wagons. The 1949 Pontiac sales folder even shows both the steel and wood models. At first glance, the steel wagons looked just like the wooden version. They had stamped outlines of wood framing on the now-steel sides and tailgate and these areas were finished with contrasting woodgrain finish. There was clearly a strong feeling that wagons had to continue to look wooden. There may also have been concern that the broad expanses of sheet metal an all-steel wagon would require would look too much like a panel truck. Thus General Motors initially kept a definite woody look. Ford continued the wood look for decades after the conversion to all-steel wagons.

Chrysler, however, took a bold step in 1949 with the introduction of the all-steel Plymouth Suburban station wagon. This was a low-priced two-door station wagon which had no pretense or appearance of wood on the exterior at all. It

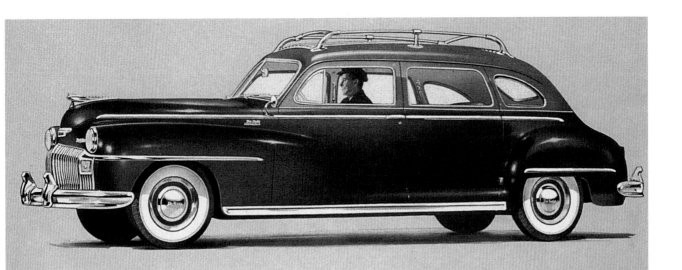

DE SOTO SUBURBAN

Station Wagon Utility... Sedan Luxury

There has never been another car like the new De Soto Suburban for town and country use. It will carry up to nine passengers, along with all of their luggage, in style and comfort. Or, if you choose, you can have more than six feet of interior luggage space, simply by moving the rear seats. In any case, you will discover a combination of practicality and smart styling that can't be matched in this handsomest of all multi-purpose cars. Like every new De Soto, the Suburban lets you drive without shifting, too. That's why you see more and more of these fine cars wherever you go.

Here is how the De Soto Suburban seats nine passengers in complete comfort and still provides substantially more luggage space than is found in conventional sedans.

The top rack, supplementing interior luggage space, features chrome railings and polished hardwood skid strips and is reinforced to hold many large pieces.

Or, with the third seat folded into the floor, and the second seat moved forward, three ride comfortably in front and more than six feet of space is free for luggage.

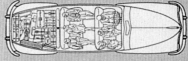

When the need is for less passenger space and more room for luggage, the third seat can be shifted in an instant, still leaving accommodations for six passengers.

The back compartment, shown with the third seat folded into the floor and the empty second seat pushed forward, provides six feet of space for luggage or for a double bed.

Luxurious Suburban interiors include smartly tailored seats upholstered in remarkably durable plastic fabric and natural wood-grained panelling with extreme resistance to flame and scuffing.

The 1946 DeSoto Suburban was an effort to provide station wagon flexibility and capacity using an eight-passenger limousine body instead of a specially built wood wagon body. The Suburban was probably the first user of a folding seat in the station wagon field. With the third seat folded and the second seat slid forward, there was a six-foot-long wood-paneled cargo area available. *Byron Olsen Collection*

A Mercury in a scene from the sales catalog of 1942. World War II was under way, so 1942 auto advertising often featured a military theme to demonstrate the patriotism of the manufacturer. The body was built of maple framing with birch or gumwood panels. Upholstery was genuine leather in a choice of red, tan, or blue. *Byron Olsen Collection*

The 1941 Buick Special Estate wagon. Buick entered the wagon market with a bang in 1940 and from then until the end of wood wagon production in 1953, produced the most glamorous and luxurious wagons in the industry. The 1941 wagon was built on the Special chassis and was powered by a 115-BHP OHV straight-eight engine. Dual carburetors were optional and added 10 horsepower. *Byron Olsen Collection*

A gleaming new 1946 Oldsmobile 66 station wagon. That meant it was the Sixty series with a six-cylinder engine. The Deluxe versions were available with genuine leather upholstery. Body construction was all wood with fabric-covered roof. *Byron Olsen Collection*

was successful right from the start and really opened America's eyes to the practical possibilities of the station wagon design. The public proved very accepting of wagons without woodwork. Still, the stylish aspect of wood took a long time to die out.

The 1949 Plymouth Suburban is sometimes regarded as the first all-steel station wagon. As we have seen, the Jeep wagon preceded it by three years and really deserves the title. Still others think the Chevrolet Suburban CarryAll dating back to the mid-1930s deserves to be first. However, this for a long time was a clumsy truck that did not appeal to most car buyers. The Packard Station Sedan also deserves to be included in this select group of steel station wagon pioneers. The Packard preceded the all-steel Plymouth Suburban by a full model year and was actually in production by late 1947. The Packard had a steel roof and almost entirely steel structure except for the wood-trimmed tailgate. This car preceded the nearly all-steel

full-size station wagons of all the other major car manufacturers by a full model year.

There was another contender for the title of the first all-steel station wagon. Crosley Motors of Cincinnati, Ohio, tested the postwar marketplace demand for an automobile of maximum economy and minimum size. CEO Powell Crosley Jr. made his money manufacturing refrigerators and radios, but had long nurtured a dream to offer Americans a basic low-cost economy car. Production began in 1939. Crosley Motors resumed production with the end of World War II and was reasonably successful for a time. In 1947, an all-steel two-door station wagon was introduced. The car had embossed side panels simulating woodwork, but was of all-metal construction, much like the Jeep wagon. These cars were truly diminutive. The wheelbase was only 80 inches, the overall length 145 inches and the weight a mere 1,300 pounds. Many a Crosley was carried by college student pranksters to strange places. Interior

33

De Luxe Metal Station Wagon
STARLIGHT BLUE

Here's Pontiac's first all-metal station wagon. It still showed lots of what appeared to be wood, but was actually a woodgrain finish applied to the steel sides. The same 1949 Pontiac sales folder also showed an almost identical wood station wagon. The wooden version disappeared early in the model year. Pontiacs were powered by your choice of straight-eight or straight-six L-head engines. *Byron Olsen Collection*

furnishings and equipment were minimal and the engine was a mere 44 CID mustering a minute 26-horsepower. The wagon version had two doors plus a tailgate and sold reasonably well at first. But by 1952, the marketplace had answered Powell Crosley's question with a resounding "no!" and production of the Crosley automobile ceased.

The Packard Station Sedan also pioneered another breakthrough feature that eventually contributed immensely to the popularity of the modern station wagon. That was the folding rear seat. The Plymouth Suburban also offered a folding rear seat, which was a major factor in its popularity. Until this time, the second and third seats of station wagons had to be unbolted and physically wrestled out of the car. It took time and was genuine work. Plymouth was not the only manufacturer to introduce folding seats in 1949. The Kaiser Vagabond and Traveler, a pioneering hatchback design, also offered a folding rear seat. Oldsmobile and Buick were the only General Motors manufacturers to introduce folding rear seats in 1949. However, none of these folding seat innovators seemed to realize what a breakthrough this would prove to be. Sales catalogs hardly mention this design feature. The folding second seat made ulitlization of the wagon interior space much more convenient.

Encouraged by the success of the Plymouth Suburban, Chrysler put into production during the 1950 model year a large all-metal four-door station wagon body for use by Dodge, DeSoto, and Chrysler Dvisions. Like the Suburban, there was no exterior woodwork,

real or bogus, whatsoever. There was, however, a good deal of wood used inside these wagons in the cargo area. Chrysler Corporation had also introduced new wood-trimmed steel-bodied four-door station wagons on all four of its marques for 1949. These new wagons all had steel roofs, steel inner sides and steel tailgates. But there was still lots of exterior woodwork on the sides of these 1949 models, because Chrysler continued to build cars with separate rear fenders. By 1950, Chrysler had adopted the folding rear seat to all of these wagons and introduced another wagon innovation that would eventually sweep the industry: the roll-down or disappearing tailgate window. By the end of the 1950 model run, Chrysler had put its all-steel station wagon body into production and phased out forever the wood-body counterparts.

The conversion to steel happened very swiftly and was almost complete by 1952. The new generation of Ford and Mercury wagon bodies introduced that year were of all-steel construction. The only wood remaining were some strips tacked on to the sides of the top-line models. All GM A-body wagons continued to use woodgrain trim, but it was woodgrain painted onto the steel. Only Buick, which continued to build a wagon body on the larger General Motors C-body, still used wood to any extent. This wagon body was introduced in 1950 and had a steel roof and some steel inner side panels. But these Buicks, which were built through the 1953 model year, still used substantial quantities of wood in the tailgate and rear corner posts and thus must be regarded as the last true woody.

34

This is a somewhat exaggerated view of Packard's unique 1948 Station Sedan. The wood shown was real but had little structural function, thus making this one of the first steel station wagons. Another innovation was a folding rear seat. *Byron Olsen Collection*

One of the all-steel wagon pioneers, a 1946 Willys Jeep station wagon. Panels were stamped with minimum curvature to reduce tooling costs. The ribs stamped on the side were intended to increase the strength of the flat panels, but were painted tan and brown to create a wood-paneled effect. Early Jeep wagons were two-wheel drive and powered with the Jeep four-cylinder engine. *Byron Olsen Collection*

Another pioneer all-steel station wagon and hands-down winner as the most compact: a diminutive Crosley, seen here after its first facelift. Note the ribs stamped on the rear side panels and painted to simulate wood. Crosley grills sometimes sported a spinning airplane propeller, further adding to the toy effect created by the tiny size of the car. *MBI Publishing Company*

As further evidence that the wood station wagon had become a style statement, the 1940s witnessed a wondrous but brief proliferation of wooden-bodied automobiles. Chrysler's first Town and Country wagon introduced in 1941 used the interior layout and steel roof panel of an eight-passenger sedan. The sides of this first Town and Country were wood paneled in the station wagon model and the trunk doors were also made of wood. Two side-hinged, curved wooden doors, much like a junior panel truck, enclosed the trunk.

The 1941 and 1942 Town and Country was a very successful style statement, but it also introduced concepts that demonstrated how the wagon idea could offer more flexible use of interior space. On the nine passenger model, the middle seat could be folded forward much like limousine jumpseats to get it out of the way. Unlike folding limousine seats, this was a bench seat with a rather short backrest and was not really comfortable for long trips. Once the middle seat was folded, the third seat could then be slid forward on tracks in the floor, thus greatly expanding the cargo space in the trunk. There was no rear package shelf or bulkhead between the passenger area and the trunk, so bulky objects

could be loaded through the rear doors and pushed forward into the passenger area. A piece of netting could be attached behind the third seat to serve as a flexible package tray. This interior configuration inspired the postwar DeSoto Suburban. DeSoto placed the sliding seat in the middle and the folding seat at the rear.

These prewar Chrysler Town and Countrys also pioneered a significant change in wagon technology. They were the first wagon-type bodies to use a steel roof, although the side construction was still largely wood. Actually, Chrysler used roof panels from their eight-passenger sedan/limousine bodies. The postwar DeSoto Suburban was really a continuation of the Town and Country idea without the wood body construction.

The Town and Country did not return in its semi-wagon form after World War II. Instead, a whole batch of wooden-bodied cars were announced by Chrysler and they were all called Town and Countrys. Chrysler intended to build a two-door sedan, a four-door sedan, a convertible, a single-seat roadster, and a club coupe. Only the convertible and the four-door sedan reached production. The single-seat convertible concept appeared in 1949 in the form of the

A Ford station wagon, circa 1950. Ford built only two-door wagons from 1949 through 1951. There is still a lot of real wood to be seen, but a closer look shows that it is all surrounded by steel.

Dodge Wayfarer Roadster, but was never produced in Chrysler form nor built of wood. The club coupe, of which six or seven prototypes were built, was actually the first hardtop convertible. When the side windows were rolled down, there was no B-post to obstruct the outlook to the sides. Unfortunately, Chrysler did not exploit this idea at the time and the first hardtops that were marketed in quantity were introduced by General Motors in 1949, which got the credit for the new body design. In spite of all the lumber Chrysler was tossing around in 1946, one thing was missing from the postwar Town and Country lineup: a true station wagon body design.

Other manufacturers dabbled with wood-bodied cars. Ford and Mercury built a wood-bodied convertible called the Sportsman from 1946 to 1948. During those years, Nash offered a fastback four-door sedan in their Ambassador series with the body constructed of wood but with a steel roof. Don't ask why—it must have seemed like a good idea at the time. These wooden-bodied Nashes were built with great care and quality and were extremely rare even at the time.

After this rash of timber cars hit the market in 1946 and 1947, one factor promptly became clear to the auto manufacturers: This was much too costly and tedious a method of building automobiles. They were all virtually handmade and probably could not be priced high enough to recover the costs of manufacturing. If they did become popular, there was no way demand could be met. Finally, nothing had been done about the poor durability of wood construction. That was doomed to lead to nothing but headaches as these cars aged.

In 1949, Kaiser Frazer introduced an innovative utility car, called the Kaiser Vagabond in its deluxe version and Traveler in its lower-priced format. At the time, Kaiser Frazer was trying to expand its model offerings on a limited budget by coming up with as many design variations based on its four-door sedan body as possible. The four-door sedan was the only body style Kaiser Frazer offered from the beginning of production until the 1951 model year. Kaiser engineers managed to come up with two four-door convertibles and a four-door hardtop as variations on their four-door sedan. Of interest to us here were the Kaiser utility sedans. The Vagabonds and Travelers were among the first users of a folding rear seat. More significantly, the trunk opening was expanded up into the roof and incorporated the rear window, thus making these cars the first true American hatchbacks. The bulkhead between the rear seat and trunk was eliminated and the entire floor area from trunk opening to the back of the front seat

All the wood seen inside and out is real, but the body structure, including the frame of the tailgate, is steel. Note how the tailgate-mounted taillights pivot so that they continue to show to the rear even when the tailgate is dropped. This is one of the last wagons to have its spare tire mounted on the tailgate.

was covered in wood with skid strips for loading cargo.

But Kaiser engineers faced one problem that their limited budget could not solve. Kaiser sedans of that era stored the spare tire upright across the back of the trunk. When Kaiser designers removed the bulkhead between the trunk and the rear seat, the spare tire could no longer be stored there. In those days, no one would think of traveling without a fifth tire, as tire reliability was nowhere near what it is today. So Kaiser welded the left rear door closed and hung the spare tire inside that door. This was a serious compromise that no doubt put off a good many buyers and squeezed the back seat to boot.

World War II created an increased awareness of the utility potential of the wagon body arrangement. Many station wagons were pressed into military and government use during the war. Several others proved useful in civilian service for carpools. Gasoline was severely rationed during World War II, so passenger capacity was at a premium. Station wagons with their eight- and nine-passenger seating capacity met that requirement beautifully.

An interesting series of station wagon conversions was carried out on Mercury and Ford sedans and coupes in an effort to get more passenger capacity for the war effort. Brooks Stevens, the noted Milwaukee industrial designer, designed a station wagon conversion to create greater passenger capacity than sedans or coupes afforded. These wagons were built by Monart Motors of Milwaukee, and utilized the sedan or coupe doors and body structure as far back as the B-post area. Coupes were turned into two-door wagons and sedans became four-door wagons. A stylish and extra-long wagon body was then fabricated of wood and hung on the back. These cars were beautifully trimmed out with wood, and in their way, foretold the future. The sedan doors were all steel and had wood strips tacked on and woodgraining applied over the steel to simulate the station wagon look and match the rest of the body, which was made out of wood. These Monart wagons were actually much sleeker in appearance than the boxy wagon bodies of the time and were very good-looking. None are known to exist today, but one would surely be a find.

Plymouth's trailblazing all-steel Suburban, seen here in 1950 trim. Introduced in 1949, the Suburban was the first car to dispense with any pretense of wood. Public acceptance was enthusiastic and real wood as part of wagon bodies would soon be history. (But not the wood look.) *Byron Olsen Collection*

The growth in popularity of station wagons brought on by the demands of World War II began to stimulate some creative thoughts among Detroit design staffs. Thinking about conversion to steel construction no doubt began at this time. If station wagons were going to become a popular body style, a construction method using something other than wood would have to be adopted. It also started designers thinking about ways to make the interior space of a wagon more readily adaptable to various configurations. An early postwar result of this thinking was the introduction of the DeSoto Suburban in 1946. This Suburban used a limousine body trimmed like a station wagon inside and equipped with a large roof luggage rack for additional cargo capacity. An innovative seating arrangement was developed to better utilize the considerable length of the eight-passenger/limousine body. The DeSoto Suburban modified the interior layout of the prewar Chrysler Town and Country and offered three full-width seats. In the DeSoto, the middle seat slid back and forth on tracks and could be run up against the front seat. The third seat could then be folded into the floor, leaving an 8-foot-long reasonably level cargo area extending from the trunk lid forward to

the back of the second seat. When the second seat was slid all the way forward, there was no room for anyone to sit in it.

The folding third seat arrangement appears to be the first use in a wagon-type vehicle of a seat which, when folded, became part of the cargo deck. The DeSoto Suburban was also innovative for a wagon-type vehicle in using an all-steel body. It carried no exterior woodwork except on the roof rack.

This was yet another variation on Chrysler's attempt to get more use out of its limousine bodies. These stretched sedans, which had room for a third folding jumpseat, were used as taxicabs, seven- or eight-passenger sedans for funeral homes, airport limousines, and even formed the basis for the luxurious Crown Imperial limousines at the top end of the Chrysler line. The DeSoto Suburban was continued until 1952. Today it is a forgotten trailblazer on the path to modern station wagons.

The end of the 1940s saw the transition from wood bodies to steel largely completed. It is ironic that Chrysler, which had championed a whole line of wood cars in 1946, had by 1951 become the first manufacturer to entirely eliminate even the appearance of wood from the exterior of all its wagons.

Pontiac's sleek and luxurious 1955 Safari, a style breakthrough in wagon design. The Safari used the Chevrolet Nomad body trimmed even more luxuriously than the Nomad. Leather and carpeting were everywhere.

CHAPTER 4
– The 1950s –

THE STATION WAGON ENTERS THE MAINSTREAM

All-steel construction and folding rear seats were the two design innovations that paved the way for the great boom in wagon popularity in the 1950s. Once these two innovations were in place, station wagon sales exploded. By the end of the 1950s, the American station wagon became the preferred and most popular family car. It had room for kids to roam around in and could haul lots of stuff, which an increasingly prosperous American family could afford to buy. These were the Eisenhower years of abundance and prosperity. President Eisenhower inaugurated the interstate highway program in 1956, which was to provide an ever-growing network of freeways upon which the American family and its new station wagon could go roaming.

But in spite of the conversion to all-steel construction, the wood look persisted stubbornly. At first, some wagons continued to use sheet metal stamped in the contour of station wagon wood framework. Often these stamped pieces were painted in contrasting colors or woodgrained with paint or a decal product produced by 3M called Dinoc. The early Willys wagon and the General Motors A-body wagons of 1949 through 1954 were notable examples of metal side panels stamped out and shaped to look like wood.

The last use of real wood on the exterior of station wagons was found in the 1953 model year. Ford and Mercury continued to tack decorative strips on their most deluxe model wagons, but while the wood strips were real, they had no structural role to play. After 1953, these wood strips were

made of fiberglass. The sides of the doors and fenders inside the wood strips were covered with imitation wood paneling made of Dinoc or similar material. However, the wood used on the Buick Estate Wagons in 1953 was more substantial. The entire tailgate, liftgate and rear window posts in the cargo area used large wood pieces or were made entirely of wood. These portions of the Buick wagon body were structural: the wood strips attached around the door windows were decorative. The 1953 Buick Super and Roadmaster Estate wagons are generally regarded as the last true "woodies."

The woody look ebbed and flowed in popularity but continued on into the 1990s. Minivans and even full-size wagons continued to offer bogus woodwork as late as the 1996 Buick Roadmaster and Chevrolet Caprice, and on the 1994 Dodge and Chrysler minivans.

Folding rear seats were one of the two major breakthroughs that paved the way for the popularity of the station wagon body style in the 1950s and 1960s. Station wagons through the 1940s required that the second and third seats be unbolted and physically removed from the car before the cargo area could be utilized for something other than people hauling. Folding seats truly made the wagon attractive on a wide scale. Converting from passengers to cargo or back again now took only a few seconds.

There were variations in seat folding mechanics. In the early versions, the rear seat bench pivoted forward 90 degrees into an upright position and the backrest pivoted down behind it. Later variations had the back seat bench pivoting 180 degrees to an upside down position and the backrest folding down behind it. This limited the height of the backrest, however. When the rear seat bench stood upright, it provided a barrier to the end of the cargo floor, which was good if you were hauling something that slid around a bit. The other arrangement made for a longer load floor, however. Eventually, some wagons adopted a third variation where the rear seat backrest simply folded down and squashed the seat cushion and locked into position. That left the legroom space for the rear seat passengers available for storage of additional cargo.

Some wagons split the back seat so that part could be folded and part could be left set up as a seat. This provided additional flexibility in configuring the interior space for passengers and cargo.

While folding second seats became universal, the third seat was a more challenging problem. The rear axle housing got in the way and over the years auto designers tried several different ways of dealing with storage of the third seat cushions. The presence of the rear axle,

The sleek rear view of the 1955 Pontiac Safari. The same tailgate ribs as used on the Chevy Nomad appear here. The slim window posts and large, curving glass areas were design breakthroughs for the time. Overshadowed by the great changes made by Chevrolet that year, the transformation of Pontiac in 1955 was equally dramatic compared to its stodgy predecessors.

Real Cargo Capacity!

The ingenious way the rear seat folds down makes a long, clear, wood-ribbed floor with the spare wheel in a tuck-away well under it. The rear deck is double-hinged so it opens up and down, clear from floor to roofline. It provides carrying space for

The Kaiser Traveler hatchback seen here in its 1951 version. The spare tire was stowed under the circular hatch in the rear floor. The skid strips in the cargo area were the only wood on the car. It was America's first hatchback, but it didn't catch on.
Byron Olsen Collection

which severely impaired foot room for a forward-facing third seat, led to the introduction of rear-facing third seats in 1957 on Chrysler products. Most other manufacturers eventually adopted this arrangement.

Rear window and tailgate arrangements have gone through a wide range of configurations in the last half-century. Most wagons started out with a lift-up transomlike rear window and a separate tailgate that lowered like a pickup truck. Chrysler introduced a rear window that rolled down into the tailgate with their 1950 wood wagons and their first all-steel wagons introduced in mid-1950. The window crank unfolded out of the tailgate handle. The window had to be rolled down free of its weather-stripping channels before the gate could be opened, which was a minor disadvantage: it took extra time. Electric operation of the window was often an option and sped up this process. By 1960, nearly all wagon manufacturers had adopted the roll-down rear window.

Here's a list of wagon manufacturers in the 1950s and the year each one adopted the roll-down rear window.

Chrysler	1950
DeSoto	1950
Dodge	1950–52, 1957
Rambler	1956 (except American)
Plymouth	1957
Mercury	1957
Chevrolet	1959
Pontiac	1959
Oldsmobile	1959
Buick	1959
Ford	1961
Studebaker	1963
Edsel	never (ceased production 1960)
Packard	never (ceased production 1958)

The roll-down rear window was not widely adopted until the 1957 model year. At that time, all Chrysler Corporation wagons and Mercury dispensed with the transom-type lift-up tailgate window in favor of the roll-down variety. Other wagon manufacturers experimented for several years with ever-wider rear windows, emulating the wraparound windshields that came into vogue in 1955. But the lift-up tailgate window, or transom, was heavy and had to be

This is Rambler's first station wagon introduced in 1950, seen here in its 1953 guise. It was built on a short 100-inch wheelbase with unit construction, and as a result, was both nimble and economical. The shrouded front wheels were a Nash trademark. *Byron Olsen Collection*

This is Rambler's first four-door station wagon introduced in 1954. This is a 1955 model with some unfortunate two-toning to compete with the wild color schemes on competitive cars that year. To save money, this wagon used sedan rear doors and the tailgate section from the smaller 100-inch wheelbase Rambler wagon. This was tied together with a stepped roof and set off with a rooftop luggage rack. *Byron Olsen Collection*

Above and opposite: Plymouth's finest wagon for 1956, the top-of-the-line Sport Suburban model equipped with roof rack. The rear view shows Plymouth's last use of a lift-up tailgate window. It also shows the first tailfins to appear in the low-price field. Chrysler Corporation led the tailfin parade in the late 1950s. The chrome wire wheels were seldom seen on wagons.

propped up when open with sturdy braces. The wraparound tailgate windows used by Ford, Buick, and Olds starting in 1957 and Chevrolet, Pontiac, and Edsel in 1958, were especially heavy and clumsy to lift.

These hefty transoms sometimes interfered with carriage of long, bulky loads that required the transom and tailgate to be left open while moving. The disadvantage of a roll-down window was that it took time to crank it down before the tailgate could be opened. A transom could be unlatched and lifted more quickly, but the roll-down window ultimately won.

Many years later, lighter, easier-to-lift rear windows would bring back the lift-up transom idea. In recent years, a variation on the lift-up transom has reappeared. In some sport utility vehicles and late-model station wagons with full-length liftgates, a separate lift-up rear

window has been provided to make it easier to reach for small objects in the cargo area without opening the entire liftgate. The large GM wagons of the 1990s also returned to the lift-up tailgate window.

In common with other body styles, interiors in station wagons brightened up dramatically during the 1950s. The plain brown leather found on a number of wagon seats in the 1940s gave way to two- and three-tone bright vinyls in the 1950s. Plastic fabrics abounded and carpeting spread throughout the passenger floor area. Wood disappeared entirely from the interiors, including the load area, and was replaced with heavy-duty vinyl floor coverings or carpet for the cargo bay.

Another automotive design trend of the 1950s, which adversely affected station wagon utility, was the move toward lower, longer

The Crestline Country Squire

This is Ford's handsome Crestline Country Squire for 1953. This was the last year Ford used genuine birch or maple for the trim strips on the sides. It was also the last year of production for the legendary Ford flathead V-8 engine. *Byron Olsen Collection*

designs. By the end of the 1950s, interior height was much reduced and this in turn made it difficult to squeeze bulky cargo into station wagons. To be sure, the floor area had increased, in some cases dramatically, but the lower roofline was a definite tradeoff.

All Chrysler Corporation wagons dispensed with any appearance of exterior wood by 1951. These were the first passenger car–based station wagons that were all steel and proud of it, because they made no pretense of looking like wood. However, they still had a lot of nice woodwork inside on the side panels and floor, which was trimmed with bright metal skid strips to keep the cargo from scuffing the varnished floor. The manufacturers may have had some concern that a wagon with no wood decoration to break up the broad expanse of exterior metal would look like a panel truck. But the public didn't seem to care.

The previous chapter described the introduction of the first true hatchback by Kaiser Frazer and its use of a folding rear seat. Although the Kaiser Frazer hatchback body did not make a great impact on the marketplace, that failing had more to do with lack of popularity of this struggling independent manufacturer than it did the merit of the body design. The idea of making the space in a sedan more flexible for utilitarian purposes did get noticed. In 1950, DeSoto began offering a sedan called the CarryAll, which was patterned after the Kaiser Vagabond and Traveler. The DeSoto CarryAll had a folding rear seat and skid strips over a handsome wood floor intended to carry cargo. When the rear seat was folded, long cargo could be loaded from the trunk all the way through to

the front seat. However, unlike the Kaiser, these cars did not have a hatchback rear trunk opening. The CarryAll was continued through the 1951 model year, but saw few sales.

DeSoto was also offering a regular station wagon from 1949 on, as well as the unique DeSoto Suburban, which had been introduced in 1946. This latter model was a limousine body trimmed like a station wagon inside and was described in the previous chapter.

DeSoto was joined by Chrysler in offering a folding seat sedan also on the six-cylinder 125-inch wheelbase chassis in 1951. Like the DeSoto CarryAll, the Windsor Traveler offered a wagon-like interior, folding rear seat and cargo floor with protective skid strips, and no bulkhead behind the rear seat. As evidence that Kaiser's innovative Vagabond had struck a nerve, Chrysler's Traveler even offered the alternative of stowing the spare tire mounted inside the left rear door just as Kaiser had been forced to do in its Vagabond. But Chryslers and DeSotos of the same era stored the spare tire upright at the side of the trunk. Therefore, when turning the sedan into a utility configuration, the spare tire was not really in the way. Yet Chrysler, on the 1951 Windsor Traveler, felt compelled to offer the alternative of getting the tire completely out of the trunk and putting it inside the rear door just like the Kaiser Traveler and Vagabond. Leaving room for the spare tire by the left door meant the rear seat had to be narrower.

Whether buyers showed any interest in this moderately strange option is unknown, but the Traveler sold only 850 copies. DeSoto's version, the CarryAll, sold 3,900 units in 1950 and 1,700 for 1951. This sales rate was not sufficient to

A handsome 1954 Mercury Monterey eight-passenger station wagon. The woodlike strips on the side were now fiberglass, but Ford Motor Company had clearly committed itself to continuing the wooden wagon look. This was a particularly attractive year for Mercury with its first OHV V-8 engine and, for the first time in the medium-price field, ball joint front suspension. *Byron Olsen Collection*

carry either the Traveler or the CarryAll into the 1952 model year offerings. Both were dropped, as was the DeSoto Suburban, leaving only the steel-bodied station wagon available in both DeSoto and Chrysler lines. The wagon made more sense because it had as much floor space as the sedans and a lot more cubic capacity for load carrying.

Nash introduced its first station wagon on the compact Rambler chassis in 1951. It had a bit of a wood look but was actually all steel and unit construction to boot. The sheet metal around the windows and on the tailgate was finished in a woodgrain pattern on some models.

The Rambler wagon was offered at first only as a 100-inch wheelbase two-door. In 1954, it was joined by a four-door version on a 108-inch wheelbase. The Rambler was a compact car built on a compact wheelbase and thus did not have very much cargo capacity. But it was well equipped, had a folding rear seat, and was quiet and rattle free because of its unit construction. It was an important step toward making wagons

Car manufacturers were continually experimenting with seat folding arrangements to provide access to a third seat in the rear. This 1954 Mercury has a split folding second seat. The narrow seat being touched by the man could be folded individually for access to the third seat, which could also be folded into the floor. But there isn't much foot room for those third-seat passengers. *Byron Olsen Collection*

A 1956 Rambler Cross Country hardtop station wagon, a body-type-first for American Motors. Although the hardtop wagons never sold very well, the regular wagons using this body were produced through 1962 and helped American Motors achieve some of its most successful sales years. *Byron Olsen Collection*

more carlike and economical. This body was dropped after 1955, and then resurrected in 1958 for several more production years as the Rambler American.

Nash Rambler introduced its first four-door wagon in 1954. It used the doors from the sedan, and a tailgate and rear roof section from the smaller two-door wagon body. The use of these components saved money in tooling up this larger wagon. They were put together on the longer 108-inch wheelbase and tied together with a distinctive dipped roof panel. Nash filled the dipped area in the rear of the roof with a standard-equipment roof rack. That rear-mounted roof rack and dipped roofline became a trademark of Rambler wagons for years to come.

Ford and Mercury wagons were all steel starting with the new body design introduced in 1952. But both Ford and Mercury continued to tack on real wood strips for two more years on the top-of-the-line models before that last vestige of real woodwork was replaced by fiberglass strips that looked like wood in 1954.

Kaiser introduced a completely new body shell in 1951 and again offered the hatchback design. Like their predecessors, these cars utilized a sedan body rather than a separately tooled wagon. In the new body the spare tire was stored under the trunk floor. The left rear door finally became functional because it was no longer encumbered by a spare tire!

Kaiser's brother marque, the Frazer, was also offered as a hatchback in 1951 for the first time. The 1951 Frazer, the last year for that marque, was actually a heavily facelifted version of the original Kaiser Frazer body design first introduced in 1947. The Frazer hatchbacks of 1951 were called the Vagabond and were actually leftover 1949–50 Kaiser Vagabond and Traveler bodies that had not been sold. Once the leftover bodies were used up, Frazer disappeared from the marketplace.

Buick introduced new body shells in 1954 and included wagons in the intermediate-size Special and Century lines. No longer was there a wagon in the Super or Roadmaster series and no longer was there any pretense of woodwork.

Two-door station wagons began to make their appearance. The first was the Willys in 1946, followed by the breakthrough Plymouth

Suburban in 1949. The Nash Rambler wagon introduced in 1951 was offered only as a two-door at first. All Fords and Mercurys from 1949 through 1951 were available only as two-doors. Beginning in 1952 Ford offered a two-door variation of its otherwise identical four-door wagons. The two-door models were usually called the "Ranch Wagon."

Two-door wagons were offered by more manufacturers as the 1950s wore on, but were never very popular. It was simply more convenient to get stuff and people in and out with four doors instead of two. Two-door wagons largely disappeared after the 1950s.

Nearly every manufacturer introduced heavily changed body shells in either 1954 or 1955. All manufacturers were completely deserting the wood look except for Ford. Ford had always sold more wagons than anybody else and continued to do so. The top-line Ford Country Squire model continued a rather elegant (but bogus) wood treatment. The trim strips were fiberglass and the paneling between the strips, which looked like yacht deck planks, were actually decals or an adhesive product known as Dinoc, manufactured by 3M Company (T/M). The cheaper-model wagons were

not trimmed with the ersatz woodwork, only the expensive ones. That pattern of trimming the most deluxe models with woodwork continued to the end of the station wagon era.

More and more manufacturers began to produce wagons. Nash had started in 1951, Studebaker in 1954, and Oldsmobile began building wagons again in 1957 after dropping them in 1951. Chevrolet and Ford offered wagons continuously from the 1930s, as did Plymouth. Dodge and DeSoto had built wagons in the 1930s and began building wagons again in 1949, as did Chrysler.

Style was swiftly becoming very important to Detroit car designers and the car-buying public. Ford had led the way to station wagons designed to be a part of the regular car line in 1952. Now for 1955, Chevrolet introduced a stunning high-style station wagon called the Nomad. This was a two-door wagon with a unique greenhouse built on Chevrolet's highly successful brand-new 1955 model and powered by its marvelous new small-block V-8. The Nomad was inspired by an auto show concept car of the year before that was translated rather quickly into a showroom-ready production model. The greenhouse was glass all around,

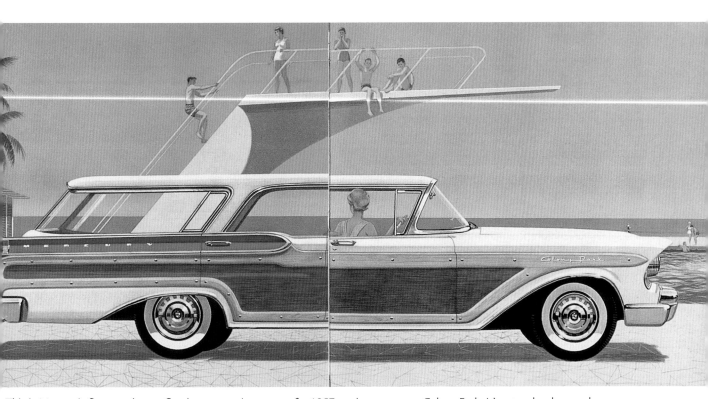

This is Mercury's finest and most flamboyant station wagon for 1957, a nine-passenger Colony Park. It's a true hardtop and demonstrates several styling fads of the day: lots of glass, a panoramic windshield with reverse-angled windshield pillar, and rocketship shapes everywhere. Mercury joined Chrysler Corporation and Rambler in offering roll-down tailgate windows with this model. *Byron Olsen Collection*

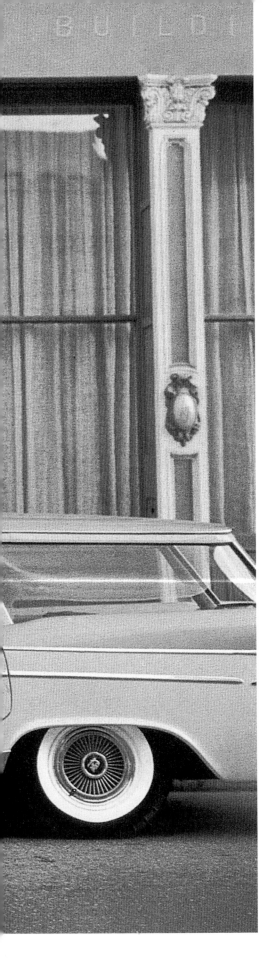

with the rear quarter windows wrapped around to the tailgate. The transom was trimmed with a light chromium frame that was quite a contrast to the heavy stamped metal liftgates on other wagons. Pontiac also used this body on its plush Safari model. Both of these wagons were produced through 1957 and made an impact on automobile enthusiasts that continues to this day. Nomads and early Safaris are highly prized on the collector car market. Never mind that two-door wagons did not develop any long-term popularity: these wagons looked just great.

Ford could not take the arrival of the Nomad without reaction. Ford had been producing two-door wagons since 1949. For 1956, in response to the Nomad, Ford introduced a gussied-up version of its Ranch wagon carrying top-line trim, fully carpeted cargo floor, and all of the chromium trim of the Fairlane series. Ford named it the Parklane. This car offered a vinyl cover that snapped neatly over the luggage area below the window line to conceal cargo, valuable or otherwise. This was an idea that caught on again many years later. But the Parklane used the regular Ford two-door wagon body, unlike the Nomad which had its own unique design. The Parklane was not repeated the following year.

Rambler became a major player in the station wagon marketplace in the late 1950s. American Motors was formed in 1954 through the merger of Nash and Hudson and introduced its first new body designs on the Rambler line in 1956. These were larger cars with significantly roomier interiors than their predecessors. Yet overall length and wheelbase remained compact. Indeed, American Motors coined the phrase "compact car" about this time. At a time when most other manufacturers were increasing the size and length of their cars, and suffering declining sales as a result, Rambler championed sensibly sized "compact cars" and kept their vehicles from growing. The result was booming sales for Rambler through the end of the 1950s and into the early 1960s. Indeed, in 1959, Rambler sales had soared to 400,000 cars, putting the company in fourth place in the sales race. Much of the success was due to large sales of station wagons that at times approached half of total Rambler sales.

The new Rambler wagon body introduced in 1956 used the same rear side doors as the sedan counterparts. This led to obvious savings in tooling and production economies. This also permitted designers to retain the by-now characteristic Rambler dipped roofline with a standard-equipment rooftop luggage rack mounted at the rear. The shrouded wheels of earlier Ramblers and Nashes gave way to full wheel openings with a wider tread. Inside, interiors were

This 1958 Dodge Custom Sierra nine-passenger illustrates the dramatic change in station wagon design introduced on all Chrysler Corporation wagons in 1957. All Chrysler Corporation wagons used this body. These cars were several inches lower than any of the competition, yet managed to provide a large cargo area with 8 1/2 feet of deck from front to rear. *Byron Olsen Collection*

Here are the kids having fun in the innovative rear-facing third seat introduced on Chrysler Corporation's station wagons in 1957. A 1957 Dodge is shown. This observation lounge "spectator" seat (as Dodge called it) provided ample leg room for third-seat passengers and yet could be folded into the floor without removing it from the car. *Byron Olsen Collection*

spacious and truly six-passenger. The wagons adopted a wind-down tailgate window and in fact were the second manufacturer to do so.

Rambler station wagons emphasized passenger car virtues and this was perhaps one reason for their great popularity. Cargo area was good, although interior height and tailgate opening height were lower than most other station wagons. The new bodies continued unit construction, which made them very tight and rattle free. An overhead valve six-cylinder engine was introduced in 1956 as the mainstay power plant, followed by a V-8 option a year later. Rambler developed a good-quality reputation in these years and resale values rose in response. The booming sales did not hurt resale either.

Rambler introduced a four-door hardtop station wagon in 1956, although these saw very low production. This was the first true hardtop station wagon with no B-post above the beltline and thus qualifies for the title of first in that category. The hardtop version used the same body shell and doors as the pillared wagons and thus cost little more to produce. The hardtop wagon was produced from 1956 through the 1960 model year, but never saw very many sales. These cars are very rare today.

To replace its discontinued Nash and Hudson big cars, American Motors in 1958 introduced a stretched version of the new Rambler body on a 117-inch wheelbase. This was called the Ambassador after the name of the top-line Nash, and was also offered in station wagon and hardtop station wagon form. Engines were more powerful and the interiors were fancier, but the Ambassador never carved out a significant market niche. The bread-and-butter car for American Motors was the Rambler Classic line, which continued to be built on a 108-inch wheelbase. The body shell introduced in 1956 was produced through 1962, which turned out to be American Motors' best years.

In 1958, upstart American Motors pulled another unprecedented stunt. AMC brought back the discontinued 1955 100-inch wheelbase Rambler with virtually unchanged sheet metal and put it back into production. To the amazement of the industry, sales of the really compact model, now named the American, also boomed, helping Rambler achieve more sales success. This compact Rambler American was built on the first Rambler platform introduced in 1950. The reintroduced line included the two-door wagon first introduced in 1951. The basic body shell, much facelifted, would continue to be built through the 1963 model year.

The hardtop body style was enjoying booming popularity and this led to the introduction of other hardtop wagons in 1957 by Buick and Mercury. Oldsmobile also reintroduced wagons into

This limited-production 1957 Pontiac Star Chief Custom Safari four-door wagon further tested the market for very luxurious station wagons, first sampled by Pontiac with the 1955 Safari two-door. This rarely seen model boasted special exterior side trim and an ultra-luxurious interior with a reclining seat. It was also known as "The Transcontinental."

The front seat of a 1957 Pontiac station wagon. The bright-colored upholstery, heavily chromed dashboard, and knee-knocking wraparound windshield are all typical for the time.

Chevy's classic Nomad two-door station wagon, here seen in the popular 1957 version. The expansive glass areas curving around to the tailgate and the distinctive chrome strips attached vertically on the tailgate are Nomad trademarks.

its model lineup in 1957 and it, too, offered a hardtop style. By hardtop we mean a body with no B-post (middle door post) above the windowsill line.

Mercury made a bold move for leadership in the growing station wagon marketplace in 1957. Mercury introduced a line of large station wagons that year, which would be continued through the 1960 model year. All were hardtops and there were no wagon models with a B-post to be found. Mercury offered several two-door wagon models during this period, although by 1960 had phased them out. These were the last years when Mercury had its own unique body shell distinct from the Ford line. From 1961 on, all Mercurys would be clones of comparably sized Ford models. But for 1957 through 1960, Mercurys were big, bold, and brash in their styling and some would even say bizarre.

The body shell Mercury introduced in 1957 was considerably larger than its Ford counterpart. In keeping with the boom in station wagons, Mercury offered no less than six new station wagons in both two-door and four-door

models and in both six-passenger and nine-passenger configurations. As previously noted, all were hardtops and all offered roll-down rear windows for the first time on any Ford Motor Company product.

The 1957 Mercurys developed a troubled reputation for poor build quality, although a number of other manufacturers had the same problem in those years. Radical design changes were coming so frequently that engineering and production staffs had little chance to get the bugs out before volume production began. Nevertheless, these big Mercurys were unique in the wagon field. With their extreme wraparound windshield, hardtop side glass, curved wraparound rear quarter windows, and roll-down tailgate window, these wagons represented an eye-catching new high-visibility outlook for wagon buyers. Floor space in the cargo area was also considerably larger than predecessor models.

These big wagons grew again for the 1959 model year when Mercurys were increased in size. It was becoming clear that two-door wagons were not selling, so the Mercury two-door offerings were reduced to one. Wheelbase went up to 126 inches and overall length to a whopping 218 inches. This large size permitted a third seat that faced forward but could still fold into the floor. It also incorporated the largest windshield ever put on any automobile. The panoramic windshield on these Mercurys wrapped around the corners and up into the roof and down into the cowl in a manner unequaled before or since. This body was continued through 1960 although the sheet metal was completely revamped. This 1960 Mercury was an uncommonly clean-lined car for the time and looks good today, except for the huge size. Never again would Mercury make a statement so distinct from its fellow cars in the Ford family.

Building hardtop station wagons was an idea that never got very far. The hardtop body style, a closed car with convertible-type windows and no B-post, got started in 1949 and took the industry by storm. Station wagon popularity was coming on at the same time. The first effort to apply hardtop window design to a station wagon was tried by Rambler with its new bodies introduced in 1956. However, Rambler was never a style leader and always got its points in the practicality parade. Rambler continued to offer hardtop wagons through 1960, but few were sold.

In addition to the 1957 Mercurys, which have already been mentioned, Oldsmobile and Buick introduced hardtop-style station wagons in 1957. Unlike Mercury, these two marques offered wagons in both hardtop and solid pillar design. The public showed no great interest in the hardtop feature and bought mostly Buick and Olds wagons with B-posts and frames

This 1957 Packard Clipper was really a Studebaker with a Packard nameplate and a few Packard trim details. It was one of the last gasps of an honored nameplate in American automotive history. Nevertheless, there was a respectable power output provided by a supercharged 289 CID Studebaker V-8 delivering 275 horsepower.

The stern view of the 1957 Packard, the first station wagon to carry the Packard name since 1948. The 1956 Packard Clipper taillights were grafted onto the Studebaker wagon body, which had been first introduced in 1954 on a more compactly sized car. The steel-framed lift-up rear window was characteristic of wagons of the day.

around the door glass. This really confirmed that the wagon buyer was a practical sort not greatly interested in the latest styling fads. General Motors caught on quickly and discontinued hardtop wagons after the 1958 model year.

Mercury, as we have seen, offered hardtop wagons through 1960 as did Rambler. Chrysler began offering hardtop wagons on its Town and Country models in 1960 and continued through 1964. Along the way, the large Dodge Custom 880 series, which used a Chrysler Town and Country body shell, also began offering hardtop wagons. Neither made much of an impact on the marketplace and hardtop wagons disappeared completely after 1964.

Chrysler introduced new bodies throughout its body range in 1957. Actually, all Chrysler products from Plymouth to Chrysler now shared the same wagon body. It was not offered as a hardtop, but all models now featured a roll-down rear window dispensing with the lift-up transom. Ford, on the other hand, enlarged the transom so that it wrapped around the sides of the body and presented a very expansive rear view.

Another interesting development in 1957 was rear-facing third seats. They were available in Chrysler Corporation wagons. These new Chrysler bodies were so low that the cargo area was diminished in height. Turning the rear seat around and placing it over the axle permitted an adequate footwell to be opened up between the rear axle and the tailgate. The spare tire had to be relocated into the fender, but the idea worked out very well. This arrangement has since fallen from favor because of the perceived risk to third-seat occupants in a rear-end collision. Nevertheless, riding backward was safer in the event of a frontal collision.

In 1957, Packard was on its last legs. A Studebaker-bodied wagon was introduced, bearing the Packard name. These were tough years for Studebaker-Packard, and the last Packard was produced in 1958. The Packard wagon was offered to the end. Studebaker introduced its first postwar wagons in 1954 and offered them continuously until the end of Studebaker in 1966.

A comparison test of four 1958 station wagons in the August 1958 issue of *Motor Trend* magazine provides an illuminating comparison of many wagon design trends of the time. The four wagons tested were a Rambler Classic, 108-inch wheelbase; a Ford Country Squire four-door; a DeSoto Fireflite; and an Oldsmobile Super 88. These cars represented a wide range in size: the Rambler was only 194 inches long while the Ford was 203 inches, the Oldsmobile 208 inches and the DeSoto a whopping 218 inches. This reflected the spread that was going on in the car market at the time. As most cars were getting larger, the Rambler was emphasizing its compact size and gaining market share rapidly at the expense of the everlonger medium-priced Detroit cars.

Rambler and DeSoto had adopted crankdown tailgate windows while Ford and Oldsmobile had gone to huge wraparound rear windows, which made for clumsy transoms. Olds would go to a crank-down window the next model year and Ford would make the switch by 1961.

All of the cars had lots of floor space in the cargo area, but not very much vertical height. Indeed, the compact Rambler could accommodate nearly as much as the Oldsmobile.

1958 Buick Century Caballero hardtop station wagon. Few automobiles built before or since have carried as much chrome and brightwork as the 1958 Buick. It was one of the last cars designed under the direction of legendary GM styling guru Harley Earl and it was clearly not one of his most tasteful efforts.

The four tested cars also demonstrated a variety of seat-folding designs. In the Rambler, the rear seat backrest simply folded down on top of the cushion. In the DeSoto and Olds, the rear seat bench pivoted 180 degrees so that the bottom of the seat became part of the cargo floor. The backrest then folded forward to fill the space left by the back seat bench. The third seat in the Ford wagon was found by the testers to be a makeshift affair with little space for passengers' feet. The DeSoto, on the other hand, accommodated three people in its rear-facing third seat in much greater comfort.

The DeSoto represented a top-line wagon with many amenities, such as an electrically operated tailgate window that could be operated either from outside or by the third-seat passengers.

The suspension on all four of these cars was judged inadequate to carry very serious loads. Prospective buyers with heavy cargo or trailers to haul were advised to buy a pickup truck! Other features: the Rambler and DeSoto had carpeting in the cargo area while Ford and Olds used a linoleum-like vinyl. The carpeting was judged more attractive. The Rambler came standard with a useful roof rack, which was an

A profile view of the 1958 Buick Caballero. Note the pillarless hardtop construction, offered by Buick for the last time in this model. The vast swathes of brightwork are accentuated in this example by chromium wire wheels. Overly decorated designs like this helped fuel a buyer revolt in favor of smaller, more cleanly styled automobiles in the late 1950s.

option on the other cars. The DeSoto's top had no ribs or reinforcing members and actually was deflected going through a car wash. The huge flat roof of the DeSoto obviously needed some structural assistance.

The testers spent some time evaluating how comfortable the cars would be to sleep in, something we don't hear much about nowadays. Except for the Rambler, these were big cars. Mileage for the group ranged from 12.7 miles per gallon to 15.7. The testers made no attempt to measure acceleration or top speed. Rambler, with its unit body frame construction, was found to be more superior to the others in terms of body tightness and freedom from rattles and twisting. Shades of things to come: by the 1990s, most passenger cars were built with the unit construction method.

The dimensions of the cars tested demonstrated how low they had become. The rear opening height ranged from 25 inches to a maximum of 30 inches—only 2 1/2 feet. This limitation on vertical access to the cargo area would lead in the 1960s to growing popularity of small vans and pickup trucks. The overall lengths also demonstrate what was

The heavy use of brightwork in the 1958 Buick extended to the interior, although the black upholstery in this example tones down the glitter. Note the absence of the B-post and the extreme intrusion of the A-post caused by the wraparound windshield.

This 1959 Rambler Cross Country represented one of the best sales years for AMC and a year in which station wagon models comprised nearly 50 percent of Rambler sales. These cars were well built, roomy, and economical, and found favor with thousands of American families.

happening in this lower and longer era. With the exception of the compact Rambler and Studebaker, U.S. wagon overall lengths ranged from 208 inches all the way up to 220 inches for a Chrysler New Yorker Town and Country. This far exceeds car lengths today: the Mercury Sable, one of the largest wagons available in 1999, has an overall length of only 199 inches.

General Motors redesigned all of its bodies for 1959. Following Chrysler's lead of two years before, all of the General Motors marques offering a wagon used the same body shell. Only

Chevrolet offered a two-door version. All of these new wagon bodies were very low, like the Chrysler bodies of two years before, and were in fact inspired by the 1957 Chrysler Corporation redesign. All of the GM bodies now adopted a roll-down tailgate window. By 1959, only Ford, Edsel, and Studebaker continued to use a lift-up, transom-type rear window.

The Edsel made a brief appearance on the station wagon scene. The wagon versions used Ford bodies and shared all of the Ford wagon principle features during the three model years of Edsel production—1958, 1959, and 1960.

The cargo end of the popular 1959 Rambler station wagon. Note the signature stepped roofline and rear-mounted roof rack. The square-cut rear design and vertical tailgate made for more cargo room inside.

The styling of the 1959 Ford was a refreshing contrast to the rocket-inspired designs of the competition. The public responded and Ford outsold Chevy, something that seldom happened in the 1950s. This Country Sedan shows the distinctive large curved glass tailgate window, which had to be lifted up for access to the cargo area. Most of the competition had switched to windows that rolled down into the tailgate. *Byron Olsen Collection*

A 1960 Mercury Colony Park showing off its true hardtop design and roll-down rear window. This was the last year Mercury had its own body not shared with any other members of the Ford family. These wagons were over 18 feet long and had cargo decks over 8 feet long with the seats folded and the tailgate closed. *Byron Olsen Collection*

CHAPTER 5
– The 1960s –

THE STATION WAGON BECOMES THE FAMILY CAR

After the soaring fins and garish two-tone paint jobs of the 1950s, American automobile design soon settled down in the 1960s. Quickly gone were outlandish and bizarre shapes with fins and blades sticking out. Gone, too, were the extremely low designs of the late 1950s, which heavily compromised interior room in station wagon form. Full-size American automobiles actually became a bit taller and, in some cases, shorter. Part of this was inspired by a growing tide of economical imported cars led by the Volkswagen Beetle. This led Detroit to counterattack in 1960 with its own compact cars—the Ford Falcon, Chevrolet Corvair, and Plymouth Valiant. The mid-1960s saw the U.S. volume manufacturers adding a whole range of intermediate-sized automobiles to their line-ups. These intermediates soon became the platforms for the muscle car era, but that's another story.

The 1960s turned out to be a decade of generally pleasing automobile designs. Bill Mitchell had taken over from Harley Earl as head of styling at General Motors. His design stamp throughout the 1960s gave General Motors some of its most attractive cars in years. Led by the clean-cut and slimmed-down Lincoln Continental introduced in 1961, Ford designs of the mid-1960s were some of the best ever seen from that manufacturer. American Motors car lines introduced in the mid-1960s were also very attractive. Only Chrysler Corporation floundered at first, as chief designer Virgil Exner found it impossible to match his earlier successes at Chrysler. After some truly bizarre designs, particularly on Dodge and

The 1960 Nomad four-door, Chevy's last fling at 1950s flamboyance. When introduced in 1955, Nomad had its own unique body, but by 1960, the Nomad name was used for the top-line standard station wagon.

Plymouth in 1960, 1961, and 1962, Chrysler Corporation got itself handsomely straightened out by 1965.

All in all, the 1960s were a golden age for automotive designers. Gasoline was cheap, and Americans seemed to continually want more power and performance. They also continued to want large vehicles and Detroit gave them their wish.

The 1960s were a performance era and saw the introduction of muscle cars led by the Pontiac GTO in 1964. Engine sizes continued to grow and performance options became more widely available, even on big cars. But this performance orientation often did not extend to station wagons. It remained difficult to buy a four-speed manual transmission, for example,

on a station wagon even when the sedan and convertible siblings offered the option.

Wagon buyers were presented with new choices in wagon sizes that had not been previously available. In 1959, most marques offered only one size: big. But by the mid-1960s, buyers had a choice of two or three different sizes of station wagon bodies from the most popular manufacturers.

After a brief fling with true hardtop wagons, this variation on the station wagon body type faded away after 1964. Dodge and Chrysler were the last producers of this body style.

During the early 1960s, imitation wood trim appeared on fewer wagons, but never disappeared entirely before enjoying a resurgence later in the decade. Ford in particular continued to champion woodlike side trim on its top-line Country Squire model. Big brother Mercury did the same on the top-of-the-line Colony Park wagons. The wood side trim consisted of pieces of fiberglass shaped and grained to look like wood strips attached to the doors and fenders. The side panels inside the strips were covered usually with woodgrain plastic sheets or decals. Some marques surrounded the woodgrain panels with bright metal trim instead of simulated wood framing.

As the 1960s wore on, more and more marques began to add wood decoration, apparently in an effort to emulate Ford's success in selling wagons. Ford consistently outsold everyone else with its wood-look Country Squire, and this continued into the 1970s.

All GM wagons for 1959 and 1960 were built using the same body shell. It was very low and, like many of its competitors, offered less useful cargo room because of the reduced interior height. Most other wagons by this time were guilty of the same offense.

Ford introduced a new body shell for 1960 that was notably longer and lower than its predecessor. It was the last year that Ford used the lift-up rear window: for 1961, even though the

A handsome 1960 Pontiac Safari, the second year of the "wide track" design. Note the huge windshield wrapping around the corners and into the roof.

body shell was continued, the rear window was converted to the roll-down variety.

The last year Mercury built cars using its own unique-to-Mercury body shell was in 1960. After that, Mercurys were made with Ford body shells, whether full-size models, intermediate, or compact. This practice continued into the 1990s.

The Big Three manufacturers, GM, Ford, and Chrysler, in 1960 each introduced so-called compact cars for the first time to supplement their full-size car lines. They were the Ford Falcon, the Chevrolet Corvair, and the Plymouth Valiant. Although they were pretty good-sized by today's standards, they were considered small and quite a breakthrough at the time. Ford and GM followed two very different philosophies in designing the new compact cars. Ford took a conventional (some would say dull) approach with an inline six-cylinder engine, rear-wheel drive, unit body, and very plain styling and trim. Chevrolet, on the other hand, was led by Ed Cole, who loved innovation. Chevy's Corvair was an air-cooled rear-engine six-cylinder car, which was very novel to say the least, for the U.S. market. It was inspired by the air-cooled rear-engine Volkswagen, which had become popular. All over the world, only GM at the time could succeed with a technological deviation from the norm of this magnitude. Other car builders could not dare to be different because of GM market domination. As it was, the Corvair never achieved great success and soldiered on through

The stern of a wide-track 1960 Pontiac Safari. There is more wraparound glass here and the rear window now rolls down into the tailgate.

The 1962 Chevrolet Corvair Lakewood station wagon. The low-slung design coupled with the rear-engine location limited cargo room and kept sales down. The Corvair wagon was built for only two years and survivors such as this one are rare indeed.

the decade under increasing criticism. It was finally scuttled by claims that its handling was unsafe, an allegation first asserted by citizen watchdog Ralph Nader. Although these claims were eventually largely discredited, by 1969 the Corvair car was dead.

Chrysler's approach to the compact car used a conventional drivetrain, but rather wild styling to set it apart from the plain-Jane Falcons. The Plymouth Valiant and, later, its Dodge Lancer clone, did use an innovative new engine design: the now famous Chrysler Slant Six. This engine was designed primarily for these two compact cars.

Both Plymouth Valiant and Ford Falcon offered wagon versions right from the outset. It took Corvair a bit longer because of the Corvair's rear engine location. The engine housing cut into the cargo area. Corvair introduced a wagon in 1961. At the same time Buick, Oldsmobile, and Pontiac introduced intermediate-sized models: the Buick Special, the Oldsmobile F85, and the Pontiac Tempest, and they all offered wagon body styles. It was clear wagons were becoming very popular indeed. Any manufacturer with offerings in the lower price ranges had to have a station wagon in its lineup.

The newly introduced Jeep Wagoneer, here shown in two-door form. As this view from the sales catalog shows, Jeep was now aiming at the family wagon market. The Wagoneer was available right from the start with two- or four-wheel drive and independent front suspension, whichever drive system was chosen. This car marked the true beginning of the SUV boom. *Byron Olsen Collection*

A 1963 Studebaker Lark Wagonaire demonstrating its unique sliding roof. The step hanging down from the tailgate pivoted out of the way when the gate was folded. These cars could be powered with anything from an OHV-6 to a supercharged V-8. *Byron Olsen Collection*

Introducing
the all new **VISTA-CRUISER**

The 1964 Vista-Cruiser, Oldsmobile's first glass-roofed station wagon. This view from a sales catalog with the Vistadome train in the background leaves no doubt as to the source of inspiration for the body style. *Byron Olsen Collection*

Ford's first compact car of the postwar era, the Falcon. This is a 1965 model and still uses the original Falcon body first introduced in 1960. The fenders have been fattened up and squared off in tune with the style trends of the day and the car now sports much more luxurious trim. This wagon is even powered by a small-block V-8 engine, a far cry from the economical six-cylinder engines of the first Falcons.

A Checker Marathon station wagon shown taking on some stylish duties. By this time, Checkers were powered by Chevy 6s and V-8s. This wagon had a large cargo floor area with room for a 4x8 piece of plywood to lie flat inside with the tailgate closed. *Byron Olsen Collection*

Full-size Chrysler products introduced new bodies in 1960 with wagons available across the board.

The first American minivan debuted in 1961. Volkswagen had been selling a clever idea, the so-called Microbus minivan with rear-engine, rear-wheel drive for years. The new Corvair and Corvair Greenbrier with their rear-mounted air-cooled engines clearly were influenced by Volkswagen success, both the Beetle car and the Microbus minivan. The Corvair Greenbrier was somewhat larger than the Microbus, but had the same basic layout with

air-cooled rear engine and a pair of side-opening doors on the right side only. The rear opening used a pair of side-hinged doors much like a panel truck.

Ford quickly followed with its version of the minivan, although they weren't called that then. The Ford Econoline "Station Bus" was completely different in layout, however, from the Corvair. It had a front engine under a cover between the front seats, and rear-wheel drive. This meant the floor was high off the ground to clear the drivetrain and the entire vehicle was also high. It was built on a very stubby chassis

Rambler's clean-lined new wagon design for 1963. This shows Rambler's unique cargo door supplied only when a third seat was ordered. Unlike the later Ford doorgate, this door could not be folded down like a tailgate. *Byron Olsen Collection*

and had short overall length. Dodge also introduced its version of the minibus, which had a drivetrain layout like the Econoline, but offered two wheelbases and was a more attractive vehicle.

This was America's introduction to the minivan concept. In typical Detroit fashion, however, these vans soon began to grow and developed into the large vans still sold today by the Big Three automobile manufacturers. These vans are popularly used in the late 1990s as the basis for recreational vehicles and high-capacity small buses capable of carrying 15 passengers or more.

The Corvair Greenbrier was the most innovative and most attractive of these early minivans. It offered reasonable performance, unlike the Volkswagen, which could not hold the speed limit in the face of a headwind. But the Corvair was doomed and the Greenbrier along with it. Over time, the engine location in the Ford and the Dodge was moved from between the front seats to a position forward under a short hood. Chevrolet followed suit, and this first generation of compact, really high-capacity vehicles grew up to become trucks. It would remain for Chrysler Corporation to reinvent the modern minivan with front-wheel drive, compact overall size, and carlike handling in 1984.

In 1961, General Motors introduced an entirely new line of full-size body shells, which as a group were very handsome and well-laid-out. The wagons looked particularly good whether wearing Chevrolet, Pontiac, Oldsmobile, or Buick trim. At that time, Pontiac was

pushing its so-called wide track, and the wide stance made the wagons look particularly competent and roadworthy.

Chrysler had introduced new full-sized bodies in 1960 and then radically facelifted them in 1961. In the eyes of many, both Dodge and Plymouth were odd-looking both years. In 1962, Plymouth and Dodge were downsized in what was a gross misreading at the time of marketplace trends. They were about a dozen years too early for the downsizing that followed the energy crisis of the 1970s.

Each year of the 1960s saw the introduction of new lines of cars in varying sizes. Chevrolet introduced the Chevy II series in 1962, which was later renamed the Nova. This was an effort to supplement Corvair sales, which were already running into trouble. The new Chevy II line included a boxy and commodious station wagon to replace the Corvair wagon. While interesting, the Corvair offered limited cargo capacity, was not popular, and was only built for two years. The rear-engined Greenbrier minivan, however, was continued for a few more years.

Third seats, for the most part, adapted a rear-facing layout. This permitted adequate leg room for passengers larger than kindergartners in the third seat. However, it was not easy to climb over the tailgate to get into the back seat. Ford dealt with this in 1966 by introducing the two-way doorgate. This design idea, which eventually swept the industry, was a very clever arrangement of hinges and latches that permitted the tailgate

A compact Dodge Dart from 1965, available with either a slant six or a V-8 engine. If this wasn't big enough, Dodge had two sizes of larger wagons available. *Byron Olsen Collection*

to be either lowered as a conventional tailgate or opened like a door. In either case the rear window had to be rolled down first.

Rambler, as early as 1960, developed its own variation: it made a door instead of a tailgate standard on nine-passenger models. The window did not have to be lowered either, as the tailgate window was surrounded by a full frame. However, the door could not be lowered like a tailgate. This meant the car could not be operated with the rear end open to carry long loads. Six-passenger models continued to use a roll-down rear window and a drop-down tailgate.

Other manufacturers were trying other tailgate variations. The compact GM intermediates, the Oldsmobile F85, the Pontiac Tempest, and the Buick Special used a one-piece liftgate. This was a design that has since become very widespread in use and is almost universal today. There was no tailgate to get in the way of access to the cargo area. Of course, there was no tailgate upon which to rest long loads either, but that was probably a lesser disadvantage.

For a time, many manufacturers offered two-door wagons, usually as a variation of four-door models. Two-door wagons have been around since the Fords and Mercurys of 1949,

the Ford Ranch wagon of the early 1950s, and Chevrolet's Nomad starting in 1955. In the later 1950s and early 1960s the two-door model was usually the cheapest wagon variation available. They were seldom very popular and gradually faded from the catalogs of the car-based wagons by the mid-1960s.

In a little-noted introduction, Willys introduced the Wagoneer in 1963. This was a boxy, compact but commodious station wagon and it was available with either two doors or four doors. More significantly, it was available with four-wheel drive as an option. It was more carlike in layout and trim than its predecessor, the trail-blazing all-metal Jeep wagon that dated back to 1946 and had been built continuously through 1962. The new Wagoneer design was a very significant automobile. Like the first Jeep wagon, it was designed by industrial designer Brooks Stevens and was a classic of straight-line, clean-cut, functional design. The car was so successful and the design worked so well that it was built with no body changes until 1991, a production span of almost 30 years—unheard of in the American automobile industry. The design was also very significant because it was the first sport utility vehicle of the type that became so popular in the 1990s. It featured a wagon-type body with four-wheel drive, and ample creature comforts. A decent ride smoothed over the rough edges of the truck side of its character and made it very acceptable as a daily use car. It must be regarded as the true trailblazer for the SUVs of today.

Another wagon design innovation that deserved more of a chance in the marketplace was introduced by Studebaker in 1963 as the Wagonaire sliding roof wagon. To build the compact Lark introduced in 1959, Studebaker had heavily facelifted a body design that dated back to 1953. Stevens was also involved in the 1963 redesign effort and it was he who conceived the sliding roof feature that was a station wagon option. The entire roof over the cargo area slid forward to permit high, bulky loads to be carried without interference from the roof. Combined with a roll-down tailgate window, this made the cargo area large enough to haul a refrigerator standing up. The roof of the Wagonaire was a clever idea, but was never emulated by competitors. Apparently, most other manufacturers realized that wagon popularity had more to do with fashion and floor space and less about cargo volume. Studebaker continued to offer Wagonaires until the end of Studebaker car production in 1966.

A handsome 1966 Pontiac, complete with vinyl roof and eight-lug cast performance wheels. These were years when Pontiac offered a long list of performance options, all of which were available on wagons as well as the rest of the line.

For 1964, GM redesigned the intermediate bodies used by the Buick Special, Oldsmobile F85 Cutlass, and Pontiac Tempest/LeMans. Chevrolet introduced a new car line using this new body and called it the Chevelle. Typical of the times, the new bodies were bigger than the ones they replaced. Detroit still thought that every American's dream was to get a bigger car every year.

Of particular interest was a special wagon body style introduced on the Buick and Oldsmobile wagons. These models used a longer wheelbase than the other wagons in the line-up and carried a raised rear roof section complete with skylights. These special models with their glass roof panels and a slightly raised rear roof section suggested the Vistadome observation sections of a passenger train. Indeed, Oldsmobile's version was called the Vista-Cruiser and one of the sales catalogs promoting the new body showed a train with Vistadomes in the background. Buick's version was called the Skylark Sportwagon.

While these models were slightly longer and had a slightly raised rear roof section permitting a bit more cargo to be carried, the Vista-Cruiser roof was primarily a style gimmick. The wheelbase and overall length of the glass-roof wagons were 5 inches longer than the standard wagons. The roof was also 2.3 inches higher. The asserted reason for the roof design was to permit the third seat to face forward. With the raised roof section and the glass roof panels, the third seat could be placed at a higher level and offer a bit more foot room than it might otherwise. The second seat was split in the middle so that the right half could be folded forward for access to the third seat. It was an interesting idea and certainly anything that brought more light into the interior was probably a good thing. The idea persisted into the 1990s when GM had its last fling at full-size station wagons. The Oldsmobile Cruiser and Buick Roadmaster Estate Wagon, introduced in 1991, once again featured a glass windshield-like roof panel over the rear seat. It was little more than a styling

Chrysler's handsome and huge 1968 Town and Country three-seat station wagon. Luxuries available included a rear wiper/washer that cleaned the rear window inside the tailgate, and a second rear air conditioner for the back-seat passengers. *Byron Olsen Collection*

Town & Country 3-seat Stat

The vast cargo deck of a 1968 Chrysler Town and Country. If you ever managed to fill up all this space, there was another 23 square feet on the roof rack. *Byron Olsen Collection*

affectation, but it clearly hearkened back to the original Vista-Cruiser/Sport Wagon of 1964.

Checker Motors of Kalamazoo, Michigan, a long-time builder of taxicabs, introduced a wagon version of its long-running and very practical Checker cab design in the 1960s. The wagon was made available in a "civilian" version with moderately attractive interior trim and in a variety of colors (other than taxicab yellow). The Checker wagon body was the basis for a line of stretched airport limousine versions of the Checker cab. This was no doubt the reason for developing a wagon-type rear section for the Checker car. But it made an attractive station wagon and was sold in very small quantities for several years. The Checker wagon had a roll-down rear window and a unique power-operated folding second seat. The wagon version was introduced in 1962 and lasted until 1975, while the end of Checker production came in 1982. The body upon which it was based was first introduced in 1956.

The development of intermediate-sized cars in the mid-1960s, following the so-called compacts of 1960, meant that by 1964 a wide variety of station wagon sizes were available. Chevrolet offered three different station wagons in 1964: the Chevy II/Nova, the Chevelle (new and introduced in 1964), and the full-size Chevrolet. Ford offered the compact Falcon in both two-and four-door models, the intermediate Fairlane, and the full-size Ford. Chrysler Corporation had a similar mix of sizes available: the full-size Dodges and Chryslers, the intermediate-size Dodges and Plymouths (Coronet and Belvedere), and the compact Valiant and Dart models.

Chevrolet brought out another variation of the minivan theme in late 1964. Ford's Econoline front-engine, rear-drive van was selling well, as was Dodge's similar version, so Chevy brought out the Chevy CarryAll van, also a front-engine, rear-drive small van. It was later renamed the Sportvan. The handwriting was on the wall for the rear-engine Greenbrier, and Chevy was going with the mainstream program. However, the Chevy van was utilitarian and made no points in the style parade. In spite of this, it sold better than the Greenbrier and was more economical to produce.

Another player on the fringe of the wagon parade was the Chevy/GMC Suburban CarryAll, the original all-steel wagon. It was still built on a truck chassis and was only available with two doors and either tailgate or truck-type panel delivery rear doors. The interior was spartan and not yet moving in the direction of today's deluxe SUVs.

International Harvester continued to produce its all-steel TravelAll. This was a true four-door truck-based wagon with lots of cargo area

Above and below: The two-way doorgate, a major Ford advance in station wagon design shown here on a 1966 model, the year of introduction. The vertical handle on the right side of the tailgate actuated the door mechanism. *Byron Olsen Collection*

Ford's top-of-the-line, best-selling Country Squire from 1967. The car still showed a lot of woodwork, but none of it was real. These big Fords were wagon sales leaders in the 1960s and 1970s.

and a third seat in the back. The layout was very similar to today's Chevy and GMC Suburbans. International was trying hard to be a player in the light truck marketplace. For 1961, the TravelAll was subjected to a body sectioning, much as a Hollywood customizer would do to bring down the height of an older Detroit car. The upper part of the body was lowered on the chassis by taking out a section of metal in the middle of the side. But the TravelAll suffered from terminal ugliness, both before and after the chop job. It was finally replaced by a complete redesign in 1969.

In 1963, Rambler introduced a completely redesigned station wagon along with the companion sedan in the Classic and Ambassador lines. These bodies had very clean lines with a tall, open greenhouse area with excellent visibility resembling then-current Mercedes sedans. The unique-to-Rambler roof-mounted rack at the rear of the roof of the wagons was continued. The step-down of the roof panel was moderated so that the roof was now almost flat. The roof rack continued to be standard equipment.

The following year, the Rambler American was completely redesigned for the first time in

Here is Ford's unique side-facing third-seat arrangement. The staggered contour of the bench cushions allowed four children or two friendly adults to be seated. This is a 1967 Country Squire but the arrangement was used through the 1980s.

13 years. The wheelbase grew from 100 inches to 106 inches and interior space was greatly expanded, yet overall length only increased by 4 inches. The station wagon shared doors and doorframes with sedan running mates, by now a familiar American Motors practice. But what was more innovative was that the American used the same doors and doorframes as the larger Classic and Ambassador models. As the smallest remaining American car manufacturer, American Motors had to continually look for cost-saving production efficiencies such as this. The Rambler American station wagon was one of the most space-efficient and attractive wagons of the 1960s. It sold well and was built to the end of the decade. Unfortunately, American Motors began to expand its line and reach into the competitively crowded full-size car field. Then after 1969, AMC not only dropped the

American, but dropped the name Rambler. After that, car buyers were never quite sure how to refer to an American Motors product. In retrospect, this was probably a marketing mistake, as AMC sales in the 1970s never again approached the heady totals of the early 1960s.

All of the Big Three full-size cars were completely redesigned in 1965. For most model years, car manufacturers make do with a facelift (changes in the exterior sheet metal), but leave the interior structural panels unchanged. A new body shell means that everything is changed, inside as well as out.

A complete change in 1965 even meant new frames for both Ford and Chevrolet. Chevrolet abandoned the cruciform X-type frame it had been using since 1958 and returned to a perimeter-type frame as used by the rest of the industry. Ford developed an innovative, flexible frame with torque boxes at the corners of the body mounts. The body structure was built more rigidly while the frame was permitted to flex somewhat and play a role in absorbing road shocks. The result was an extremely quiet, shake-free ride that led the industry. Ford even advertised that their cars rode more quietly than a Rolls Royce.

With the widespread use of wagons, a problem unique to the wagon body style became evident. The rear window got messed up with mud and road dirt almost immediately when rain or snow was encountered. This was caused by reverse airflow, which is present at the rear of all vehicles at speed. The manufacturers began experimenting with various forms of air deflectors to redirect the airstream passing over the car to the rear window to blow spray away from the glass. In 1965, Ford and its almost-twin-brother, Mercury, introduced built-in air deflectors mounted at each side of the rear window. Air passing the side of the car was diverted across the back window to blow rain and soil off the rear glass. It was moderately effective, and inspired other manufacturers to try their hand at dealing with the same problem.

The new full-size wagons from Chrysler Corporation in 1965 were monumental in size, but very handsome. The same body was used on everything from the Plymouth Fury I to the

A flashy 1968 Impala wagon leaping ahead as if it just got the green light at the drag strip.

Another view of the 1968 Chevy. The long rear side windows give some idea of the large cargo area.

Chrysler New Yorker Town and Country. The latter was the most expensive American production wagon and sold for $4,856 in the nine-passenger version. Dodge also offered a variety of wagons and once again began offering simulated woodgrain siding on the highest trim level Dodge Custom 880. Inspired by Ford's success with the Country Squire, phony woodwork was beginning a slow comeback.

Ford's new 1965 wagons featured other innovations. When a third seat was offered, Ford provided two short side-facing seats instead of a single rear-facing seat. This enabled Ford to claim that their car could accommodate 10 passengers. The last four passengers, however, had to be very small in stature to all fit together in the cargo bay.

Plymouth and Dodge continued to produce the mid-size Belvedere and Coronet wagons, which had first been introduced as downsized, full-size Plymouths and Dodges in 1962. Whether because of the slightly smaller size or the bizarre styling, they sold poorly in 1962. But the basic body design was sound and roomy, and by 1965, the cars had been restyled into handsome and commodious wagons. Since they had been somewhat smaller than average to begin with, each now found itself in the intermediate category.

By 1965, the following U.S. manufacturers were offering station wagons:

Plymouth: Fury (full-size)
           Belvedere (intermediate)
           Valiant (compact)
Dodge: Custom 880/Polara (full-size)
           Coronet (intermediate)
           Dart (compact)
Chrysler: Town and Country (full-size)
Ford: Country Squire/Ranch Wagon (full-size)
           Fairlane (intermediate)
           Falcon (compact)
Mercury: Colony Park/Commuter (full-size)
           Comet Villager (compact)
Chevrolet: Bel Air/Impala/Biscayne (full-size)
           Chevelle (intermediate)
           Chevy II Nova/100 (compact)
Pontiac: Catalina Safari/Bonneville Safari (full-size)
           Tempest Safari (intermediate)
Oldsmobile: Vista-Cruiser/F85 (intermediate: no full-size wagon)
Buick: Special/Sport Wagon (intermediate)
Checker: Marathon/Superba (full-size)
Studebaker: Lark Wagonaire (full-size)
Rambler: Ambassador (intermediate)
           Classic (intermediate)
           American (compact)
Jeep: Wagoneer (SUV)

It is notable that, for the time being, Buick and Oldsmobile were not offering full-size wagons. This left the Pontiac Bonneville as the largest General Motors–built station wagon. Top-end luxury cars, such as Cadillac and Lincoln, did not offer station wagons. Occasionally, in the 1950s and 1960s, and even as late as the 1970s, station wagons were built by private body builders on Cadillac chassis, but neither Lincoln nor Cadillac ever cataloged a wagon body. Chrysler, however, had regularly offered wagons since the first Town and Country in 1941. Packard, too, had an occasional fling with the station wagon body-type before it finally went out of business for good in 1958.

The big wagon news in 1966 again came from Ford. Introduction of the innovative two-way doorgate solved the problem of convenient ingress and egress to the third seat, which was frequently ordered. Up to this time, third-seat passengers had to clamber across the tailgate to reach the seat. The doorgate could fold down like a conventional tailgate for hauling long loads by grabbing the latch at the center of the tailgate, but if one twisted the door handle on the right side of the gate, it opened like a door instead of dropping down like a tailgate. It was clever, required no tools or special training to operate, and worked very reliably. It would sweep the industry in short order, although General Motors was reluctant to admit that any other manufacturer could come up with something truly innovative. Loading some kinds of cargo was easier with a door than a tailgate, as well.

The 1969 Rambler American. This was the last car to bear the Rambler name and was one of AMC's more successful product offerings during the decade of the 1960s. It was well built, roomy for a compact car, and could be ordered with an OHV-6 or V-8.
Byron Olsen Collection

A 1969 Chevy Sportvan with seats and engine cover removed and displayed to show the interior layout. This is typical of first-generation small vans, particularly the large engine hatch taking up much of the space between the front and second seats. Although there was carpet on the floor, trim was generally plain and the vehicles were more like trucks than cars, including the front suspension. *Byron Olsen Collection*

In 1967 Chevrolet and GMC carried out a major redesign of the truck-based CarryAll Suburban. It grew inside, but assumed more wagonlike proportions and a more carlike appearance. It was still a truck and the interior trim was still well short of luxury, but the trend was unmistakable. The Suburban was slowly moving toward the wagon mainstream. The door arrangement was unusual: two doors on the right side for the first time, but still only one door on the left. This was to remain a feature of this particular body style until it was again redesigned in 1973, at which time it finally got four doors.

By 1967, more and more manufacturers were returning to the use of simulated wood exterior trim, usually on the most deluxe models in the line. Ford consistently used fiberglass strips that were covered with a light-colored woodgrain to outline an area of the side panel and tailgate that was covered with dark woodgrain simulated paneling. The top-line models of the intermediate Fairlane and compact Falcon wagons were also dressed up with woodgrain.

Mercury followed a similar course except that, from 1967 on, the top-line Colony Park used a chrome strip to outline the woodgrain applique instead of raised woodlike strips as on the Ford.

Oldsmobile and Pontiac began offering wood applique on the sides in 1967. Chevy reintroduced wood trim on the Caprice wagon in 1966.

Dodge and Chrysler also offered wood trim, as did American Motors' top-line wagons. Even the Jeep Super Wagoneer began to appear with a slim woodgrain feature strip. By 1969, just about every manufacturer was offering imitation wood trim on at least one station wagon model.

Manufacturers began offering air deflectors roof-mounted over the back window to duct air down over the rear window to keep it clean. Ford continued its side-mounted built-in air deflectors on its full-size wagons. But air deflectors were only partially effective. A better solution to the rear visibility problem would have to await the introduction of tailgate-mounted windshield wipers and washers.

The two-way doorgate introduced by Ford began to spread to other makes in 1968. Plymouth and Dodge introduced the doorgate on their intermediate wagon models as standard equipment. The two-way doorgate appeared on the redesigned full-size Chrysler Corporation wagons in 1969.

By 1969, the two-way doorgate also spread grudgingly to General Motors. Buick and Pontiac adopted it, but Chevrolet had to go one better than Ford. A step was notched out of the rear bumper and the cover for the step recess was attached to the tailgate. So when the doorgate configuration was chosen, opening the door revealed a built-in step for extra ease in climbing into the third seat. An interesting idea, but probably not worth the effort. Intermediate-size Chevrolet wagons offered only a lift-up tailgate, but Buick wagons, using the same body shell as the intermediate Chevelle, offered a doorgate.

Big Pontiac wagons also offered the Chevrolet-style doorgate with the notch cut out of the rear bumper for a step.

The Jeep Wagoneer was well established by 1969 as a serviceable, go-anywhere, four-wheel-drive wagon, and was offered with very comfortable interiors. The Jeep wagons were now trimmed like a reasonably luxurious automobile.

The new full-size Plymouth-Dodge-Chrysler station wagons introduced in 1969 offered a built-in rear air deflector. The Chrysler version ran across the top of the window and differed in that respect from the Ford air deflectors that were mounted on each side.

Oldsmobile and Buick introduced new bodies on the intermediate-size chassis, the only one on which those two marques offered station wagons in 1968 and 1969. Olds offered two styles of wagons in the new body series. One was a conventional four-door wagon and the other was a continuation of the Vista-Cruiser idea with skylights in the roof. This glass roof model was available in both Buick and Oldsmobile form. Buick called theirs the Sport Wagon and Oldsmobile continued the Vista-Cruiser name. Buick did not offer the shorter, plain-roof version in 1968 or 1969. The two glass-roof models were 5 inches longer in overall length and rode on a 5-inch-longer wheelbase. Overall size of these so-called intermediate wagons now approached that of full-size wagons of only a few years before.

As the decade ended, the automobile industry was treading water. No clear sense of design direction was evident and the drawing boards were filled with ever larger and more lavish designs. There was no hint of the energy crisis that would burst on the scene in the early 1970s. But there were a few clouds on the horizon. Each year, federal government regulations imposed additional limits on air emissions from automobile engines. This was leading to a decade of poor drivability until engineers figured out ways to manage engines to produce both good economy and low emissions. Safety requirements were being added each year as well. The stage was set for the decade of the 1970s, which would largely preoccupy the industry with meeting these external challenges.

Above and page 90: Two views of one of the largest station wagons GM ever built, in this case a 1972 Pontiac Grand Safari. The extreme taper of the tailgate glass reduced cargo room. This body was used by Chevrolet, Oldsmobile, and Buick, as well as Pontiac. This example measures a whopping 19 feet in overall length.

CHAPTER 6
– The 1970s –

TROUBLES AND CHALLENGES

When the decade of the 1970s dawned, it was business as usual for American car designers, at least in the beginning. The only style trends were ever-greater size and sharply curved side contours with rocker panels rolled under and side window glass curving sharply inward at the top. Neither trend had much to recommend it from a practical standpoint. Ever-growing size was once again trying the patience of the American motorist. And the heavily curved underside contours brought painted sheet metal into direct contact with debris thrown up by the wheels. The result was nicked side paint and early rusting.

For 1970, Buick added a full-size station wagon to its lineup, using the same bodies that had been offered for the preceding five model years by Chevrolet and Pontiac. However, Oldsmobile continued to limit its wagon line to the intermediate-sized Vista-Cruiser and Cutlass station wagons.

For 1970, all General Motors divisions offered doorgates. GM had been resistant to adopting the doorgate because it was so obviously invented by Ford. GM did not wish to concede that Ford might have had a "better idea," especially since this had been one of Ford's advertising slogans.

As the new decade dawned in 1970, there were fewer compact or small-size wagons. The main wagon market was in the full-size and intermediate car lines. The 1970 line-up looked like this:

Marque	Full-size	Intermediate
Ford	Country Squire/ Ranch Wagon	Torino Squire/Falcon
Mercury	Marquis	Montego
Plymouth	Sport Suburban	Belvedere Sport Satellite
Dodge	Polara/Monaco	Coronet
Chrysler	Town and County	
Chevrolet	Kingswood Estate	Chevelle Concours/ Greenbrier/Nomad
Pontiac	Executive Safari	LeMans Safari
Oldsmobile		Vista-Cruiser/Cutlass
Buick	Electra Estate	Sport Wagon (no more skylights)
American Motors		Ambassador/Rebel SST

General Motors introduced a completely redesigned full-size body for use by all five GM divisions in 1971. The body change cycle had been stretched considerably as the previous full-size body shells were introduced in 1965 and used for six model years. In the 1950s and early 1960s, a three-year body cycle was considered normal.

The most notable feature of the 1971 GM full-size station wagon was the introduction of a clamshell-type tailgate. Apparently still smarting from Ford's development of the doorgate, GM was trying to go Ford one better. With this new design, the rear window rolled up into the roof while the tailgate rolled down underneath the rear floor. This required several design compromises. The rear window had to be slanted extremely in order to make the bend rolling up into the roof. This reduced cargo area compared to some of the more squared-off competitors. The window had to be power operated.

Many of these wagons came with the tailgate also power operated. This turned out to be a Hobson's choice: unpowered, the tailgate was a real armful to drag back up into the closed position. On the other hand, the power-operated versions soon ran into trouble with malfunctions from jamming and sticking. Fouling of the tracks from dirt or bending happened all too frequently.

The clamshell idea caused enough problems in service so that it was not repeated the next time GM did a station wagon body redesign. The clamshell tailgate also filled up the underfloor cargo area when it was open and prevented the use of rear-facing third seats.

Top and bottom: Open and shut views of the unique GM clamshell tailgate used on full-size wagons from 1971 through 1976. This example is a 1972 Pontiac Grand Safari. Note the extreme "tumblehome" or slant of the side glass and tailgate glass. This was a styling trend of the times. Note also that the tailgate really does disappear completely, permitting more convenient access to the cargo area. However, there's nothing upon which to rest long loads.

A rare 1970 Oldsmobile Vista-Cruiser with both the 442 and W30 performance options. Rarely found on wagons, these muscle-car additions make this a particularly attractive and desirable car.

This redesigned station wagon body had other design features that did not stand the test of time well. These bodies and their sedan counterparts were very wide at the beltline. But the window area rolled sharply inward as it approached the roof. Stylists refer to this as "tumblehome." The 1970s was also the decade when rocker panels were curved in under the car. The combination of the tucked-in rockers and the sharply curved side glass gave the side of the car an airplanelike fuselage effect. But the tucked-under rockers were exposed to road splash from the wheels and soon caused premature rust-out of rocker panels and lower doors in northern climates. These GM big cars were the first new bodies from a major manufacturer in the decade of the 1970s and the design was, on the whole, unfortunate.

Oldsmobile returned to the ranks of full-size wagons in 1971 and offered a version of the clamshell wagon body on the Ninety-Eight Series 127-inch wheelbase. This was a big, handsome wagon and could take 4x8 sheets of plywood flat on the floor inside the cargo area. Four General Motors divisions were offering versions of the clamshell tailgate wagon body.

A new generation of compact cars started out in the 1970s. Chevrolet introduced the Vega with a two-door wagon body in 1971 and Ford introduced the Pinto in wagon form in 1972. Deluxe Pinto wagons were offered with bogus wood side trim and were quickly dubbed "Country Squirt," the kid brother of the big Ford Country Squire. Both Vega and Pinto used a lift-up hatch to close the rear opening. There was no drop-down tailgate. During the early 1970s, Chevrolet offered three sizes of wagons and each one had a different method of accessing the cargo area: the Chevelle continued to use the doorgate, the big Chevy used the clamshell, and the Vega used a liftgate.

For 1971, Chrysler Corporation introduced a redesigned line of intermediate-size bodies to be used on the Dodge Coronet and the Plymouth

The cargo end of a 1970 Olds 442 Vista-Cruiser wagon showing the skylights over the back seat and cargo area.

Belvedere/Satellites. Like most redesigns in the early 1970s, these cars grew in size compared to their predecessors. This continued growth in car size would soon be arrested by the petroleum shortages that began in 1973. Ford wagons continued to lead the industry in sales and the most popular model was the well-decorated (with imitation wood) Country Squire model. The intermediate-size Torino also continued the wood look on its higher-priced models and even the Ranchero, a wagon-based pickup truck, sported woodgrain siding.

During these years, Ford was the acknowledged sales leader in the station wagon field. The big Ford Country Squire, with its acres of floor space and seating for as many as 10 people (if they weren't all adults), defined what America wanted in a wagon. Ford wagon sales led the industry during a time when station wagons accounted for close to 10 percent of the market. Wagon sales were an even larger percentage of total Ford sales. In 1971, for example, Ford sold over 233,784 full-size wagons, of which the wood-trimmed Country Squire counted for a whopping 130,644 of those sales. These figures don't include the intermediate-sized Torino production, which accounted for another 60,645 sales, or Econoline van production. The arrival of the Pinto station wagon the next year added over 100,000 Pinto wagons to production totals. Clearly, Ford deserved its self-proclaimed role as America's wagonmaster. The big Fords were large, lavishly equipped cars. The Country Squire regalia gave the family wagon something of the aura of a cabin cruiser. By 1972, overall length of big Ford wagons reached 221 inches and almost 80 inches in width. Curb weight for a Country Squire exceeded 4500 pounds.

Roof racks were common, as were rear air deflectors. Some manufacturers, including Ford, offered a rear window cleaner that washed the glass when it was lowered into the tailgate. Sedan decorative trim ideas such as

The rear of this 1970 Oldsmobile Vista-Cruiser shows off two popular features of wagons of the 1970s: the air deflector mounted over the rear window to help keep it clean, and the roof-mounted luggage rack. This car also shows General Motors' version of the two-way doorgate with the unique notch cut out of the rear bumper to the right of the license plate. A small piece of bumper was attached to the tailgate and revealed a step when the gate was opened as a door. The dual exhausts and the numbers on the tailgate are a reminder that this is a high-performance wagon.

Badges of performance on a 1970 Oldsmobile Vista-Cruiser wagon. It was the last big year for muscle cars, although few wagons were equipped with high-performance options. This Olds wagon was a rare exception, and was a special-order car.

The 1976 Dodge Aspen, and its near twin, the Plymouth Volare, were intended to replace the popular Dart and Valiant models. Although an attractive and roomy wagon, early Aspens were plagued by poor build quality, which gave them a bad reputation. Power came from a choice of V-8s or the indestructible 225 CID Slant Six. As the energy crisis caused more downsizing, this platform and body were upgraded and eventually used on senior Chryslers. *Byron Olsen Collection*

vinyl-covered roofs appeared on wagons as well. Functionally, cargo area had never been greater and most full-size wagons would accommodate a 4x8 sheet of plywood laid flat between the wheelhouses. But low rooflines compromised the height of objects that could be carried. This limitation ultimately contributed to the growing popularity of vans and truck-based utility vehicles.

Big brother Mercury, with its lines of cars closely paralleling Ford, also decorated its top-end wagons with imitation woodwork. Since Mercury used the same body shells as Ford, each Mercury wagon was a near clone of a Ford running mate. The Mercury Montego wagon was essentially the same car as the Ford Torino and the Torino Squire wagons. The full-size Mercury wagon, the Marquis Colony Park, was Mercury's version of the Ford Country Squire. Mercury models, of course, used different grills and varied the other trim in order to distinguish themselves from their Ford sisters. On the wood-decorated wagons, after 1967, Mercury quit using the light-colored imitation wood strips surrounding the dark paneling area. Instead, Mercury edged the broad wood-paneled flanks with a bright metal strip.

Outside of the Big Three (GM, Ford, and Chrysler), there were few wagons available. American Motors was again struggling, but continued to produce attractive intermediate-sized station wagons on the Ambassador and Matador platform. This body design had been first introduced in 1967, but remained competitive in both style and equipment with the larger manufacturers. However, they sold poorly in the marketplace. AMC also introduced a new wagon-type body in 1971 called the Hornet Sportabout. This was a compact four-door with a wagon-shaped rear body with a sharply tapered rear end. Access to the cargo area was through a hatch, which did not, however, open down to the floor level. The Sportabout was clearly oriented more to being a car than a wagon.

General Motors redesigned its intermediate cars for 1973: the Chevrolet Chevelle, the Pontiac LeMans, the Oldsmobile Vista-Cruiser, and the Buick Century. As was common at the time, these cars grew in size compared to their immediate predecessors.

After all of GM's trouble with the complicated clamshell tailgate and its reluctance to use the two-way doorgate, these new GM intermediate bodies reverted to a one-piece lift-up tailgate. There was no longer a drop-down tailgate that could serve as an extension of the load floor. Nor was there any way to open the back window to carry certain kinds of long cargo without driving with the entire tailgate open. The liftgate did make access to the third seat convenient, for those so equipped. But it was a huge, cumbersome tailgate because these cars had grown in size. This pattern of constant increase in car size, which had been common in the American automobile industry since the ending of World War II, was about to change. The Arab oil embargoes and petroleum shortages, which first arrived in 1973, would turn around the direction of car sizes permanently.

But for now, the growth in size of Buick intermediate models illustrates the point. The Buick intermediate wagon body introduced in 1964 had an overall length of 203.5 inches and rode on a 115-inch wheelbase. While the new intermediate wagon body introduced in 1973

rode on a wheelbase only 1 1/2 inches longer, overall length had grown to 216.6 inches, an increase of more than a foot. This was a trend that was well to reverse, although the inconvenience and disruption of the recurring energy crisis was not the best inspiration.

These new GM bodies had also adapted strange side window configurations. All models now had a fixed B-post, coupes and four-doors alike, thus hardtop body design was gone forever. Yet all the body styles including the wagons used convertible-type side windows with frameless glass. This meant that side window weather sealing was entirely dependent on the roll-up windows remaining steady in their tracks. It also meant that the integrity of the side window weather stripping became much more important for weather sealing. But General Motors did not originate this somewhat inexplicable construction design change. Ford sedan and wagon bodies, both full-size and intermediate, introduced in the 1970s, also used frameless

side door glass, even though the B-posts were fixed in place.

Oldsmobile offered its version of this new body and called it the Vista-Cruiser, as in years past. But the domed roof with skylights was gone. In its place, a small glass pop-up sunroof could be ordered.

Other minor innovations that came along this year from Ford were an optional game table that could be placed between the rear side facing seats in the large wagons. Kids could amuse themselves on long trips. Ford also made available a spare tire extractor. Automobiles in those days still carried full-size spare tires in wagons and often placed them in a vertical position in a fender well behind the right rear wheelhouse. But the tires and wheels had gotten large and heavy and were difficult to lift out. Ford's extractor handle eased the task.

The arrival of petroleum shortages did not have an immediate effect on car design, because it takes manufacturers two or three years to bring a new design into production. But it did have an immediate effect on sales of larger cars. Paradoxically, full-size van sales, such as the Ford Club Wagon, were growing. Plymouth introduced its first van, the Voyager, in 1974. It was identical to the popular Dodge van. Americans were becoming less concerned with style, but more concerned with function. These big vans did a better job of hauling all the gear the prosperous American family had accumulated.

Also on the practical vs. stylish front, sales of American Motors Jeep Wagoneers and Cherokees continued to show healthy growth. So did sales of General Motors' Suburban, completely redesigned in 1973. The Chevrolet Suburban now had four doors, as well as a choice of tailgate designs. The new Suburban was offered as before with either Chevrolet or GMC labels.

Ford redid its full-size wagons in 1973 and Chrysler did the same for the 1974 model year. They were large cars, and this was unfortunate timing against the backdrop of growing world

PINTO WAGON SHOWN WITH ACCENT GROUP

PINTO WAGON SHOWN WITH SQUIRE OPTION AND LUGGAGE RACK

The 1971 Chevrolet Vega was GM's smallest wagon introduced in the 1970s. Plainly trimmed but attractive, the Vega soon developed a reputation for short-lived engines and early rust-out. The wagon was available only as a two-door. *Byron Olsen Collection*

Station wagons were popular as trailer-towing vehicles until recent years when truck-based vehicles have taken over that role. Here, a 1976 Dodge Coronet wagon is hitched-up and ready to hit the road. The intermediate Coronet could be set up with a 360 CID V-8 and other equipment sufficient to move a 5,000-pound trailer. *Byron Olsen Collection*

energy shortages, because it would be several years before either manufacturer could justify completely redesigning their full-size lines of cars to downsize them for economy. General Motors was farther along in its body cycle and thus was able to downsize its full-size cars for the 1977 model year. These 1977 changes at GM were dramatic and in fact reduced the size of some full-size wagons to less than their so-called "intermediate"-sized running mates. For example, the 1977 Buick Estate Wagon, the full-size model, was 216.7 inches long and rode on a 116-inch wheelbase. The Buick Century wagon, the supposedly smaller intermediate-sized running mate, also rode on a wheelbase of 116 inches and had an overall length of 218.1 inches, 1 1/2 inches longer! The GM intermediates were redesigned completely and downsized the following year.

At the beginning of the decade, Detroit had lost its sense of direction: the new product offerings just kept getting bigger and fancier with little significant innovation and few new body design ideas. But it wasn't long before Detroit

Mainstay big Ford wagons from the years when Ford called itself America's "Wagonmaster." Shown here is a 1973 Country sedan on the left and the lower-priced Ranch wagon in the background. Together with the wood-trimmed Country Squire, these were America's most popular big wagons in the 1970s. *Byron Olsen Collection*

was beset with growing safety and environmental regulatory requirements that increasingly usurped design and engineering talent. For example, by 1973, bumpers had to be redesigned to sustain low-speed impacts without damage. By 1974, that requirement extended to the rear of the car. Safety requirements were rampant at this point. Dashboards and interior fittings had to be nonhostile. Combination lap and shoulder belts came in. Other safety requirements were less visually evident, but nonetheless required substantial design and engineering sacrifices. Environmental concerns led to increasing emphasis on reduction of noxious emissions. Clean Air Act requirements required cleaner-burning engines.

Then in 1973, the first energy crisis undercut all of the assumptions upon which American automotive design had been based for several decades. Size and power had to be reduced instead of continually increased. The design direction had to be completely turned around. This led to a scramble through the remaining years of the decade to downsize and, at the same time, get improved fuel efficiency without compromising emission control issues. So the engineers in Detroit were faced with the dilemma of adding improved fuel economy to the previous burden of improving air quality emissions. In many cases, environmental improvements had reduced fuel economy.

At General Motors, the response to the energy crisis was led by Chevrolet. In addition to the downsized full-size cars introduced in 1977, all of the intermediate cars were downsized and completely revamped in 1978. This led to the strange anomaly of a 1978 Chevrolet Malibu being smaller than the Nova, which was supposed to be the bare-bones-bottom-of-the-barrel Chevrolet. The new Malibu averaged 193 inches overall length while the carryover Nova was some 3 inches longer. The same dichotomy had been present the year before when the downsized Caprice/Impalas first made their appearance. In 1977, the Chevelle wagon was 215 inches long while the new full-size Caprice wagon was 1 inch shorter.

All in all, the downsizing was healthy for the industry and the auto-buying public. The new downsized models generally had more interior room and fully comparable cargo capacity while at the same time offered increased economy and greater maneuverability.

This downsizing also marked a significant turning point in American automotive design. Until 1977, the overriding design trend was to

make automobiles continually larger. Each car didn't get bigger every year, but over time, they all did. This could not have continued indefinitely and it is probable that competition from more rationally sized imports would have eventually turned this trend around even without the energy crisis.

The new 1977 downsized Caprice/Impala was a handsome square-cut practical design. Wagon contours were squared off, leading to a generally more useful cargo area than its full-size predecessors. These wagon bodies were also made available in virtually identical form in Pontiac, Oldsmobile, and Buick versions. To the great relief of General Motors, the new downsized cars proved immediately popular with buyers.

Indeed, they proved so successful that they were built through the entire decade of the 1980s right through the 1990 model year. The test of the soundness of the design was demonstrated by how little change was made during 14 production years. Introduced in 1977, the big Chevy wagon was 214.7 inches long and carried a 5-liter V-8 as the standard-equipment eight-cylinder engine. Some 14 years later, the wagon had grown only one inch and still carried the 5-liter V-8 as standard power.

So successful was this wagon design that Buick and Oldsmobile continued to offer this full-size, rear-wheel-drive wagon through the 1990 model year, long after these divisions had discontinued the production of sedan counterparts of these bodies.

This new full-size GM wagon body thankfully abandoned the foolishness of the clamshell tailgate design and returned to the reliable, flexible, two-way doorgate. A roof rack with built-in rear window air deflector became standard equipment. A third seat, when ordered, once again faced to the rear. This configuration—doorgate, rear-facing third seat, and roof rack—became virtually standard on full-size wagons from most manufacturers during the 1980s.

General Motors still was not quite finished trying offbeat tailgate arrangements on station wagons. The downsized intermediate body line introduced for 1978 (Chevrolet Malibu, Oldsmobile Cutlass, Buick Century, and Pontiac LeMans Safari) shunned both the doorgate and the one-piece lift-up gate in favor of a design throwback to the 1950s. The tailgate dropped down flat but did not open like a door. And the rear window lifted up on struts rather than winding down into the tailgate. This cargo access configuration had not been seen on an American wagon since the late 1950s. The lift-up transom did differ from its 1950s vintage ancestors. It was basically just a piece of lightweight tempered glass with metal edging and was held up by gas-filled struts. It was quicker to open than cranking a window down into the tailgate and was lighter in weight than the transoms of the 1950s.

Although the tailgate was widened as much as the body would allow, there was less than 4 feet between the wheelhousings. But then, few

The unusual 1975 AMC Pacer sedan was joined in 1977 by this equally novel two-door station wagon. Complete with the usual station wagon imitation woodwork, this Pacer offered limited cargo area but huge doors for access. The right door was actually longer than the left for better access from the curb side. *Byron Olsen Collection*

Above and opposite: This Cadillac Fleetwood station wagon from 1975 proves that the era of custom-built bodies was not quite dead in the 1970s. The rear body from a full-size GM wagon of the same vintage, complete with clamshell tailgate, has been grafted on to the mammoth Cadillac Fleetwood chassis to make without question the largest and most luxurious station wagon of the decade.

people expected an intermediate-size wagon to carry uncut sheets of plywood.

There were other unusual aspects to this new design. In an apparent effort to get as large a tailgate opening as possible, the gate was brought out to the full width of the car body leaving no room for taillights. These had to be mounted in the rear bumper, a location vulnerable to damage and corrosion failure. But in other respects, the new GM intermediate bodies followed the lead of the full-size cars the year before. They were squared off and roomier than their predecessors, while at the same time being dramatically shorter in overall length. Roof racks with built-in rear air deflectors were common equipment on all of these downsized GM cars.

There were other handy touches. Storage compartments were built in to the side panels behind the rear wheels that could be locked. There was underfloor storage in the cargo area, but no third seat options. One design feature common to all of these new GM intermediates that was thankfully never repeated again were rear door windows that did not roll down in any four-door model, including wagons. The door windows were fixed in place to save a few dollars by eliminating the cranking mechanism. This was a prime example of why bean counters should never be allowed to get involved in the design process. To compensate for the inability of the back seat passengers to access fresh air, functioning rear quarter vent windows were installed. This was another throwback to the

1950s, because operating vent windows had virtually disappeared by the 1960s. But this design deficiency was always unpopular and was never repeated by General Motors nor copied by other manufacturers. Nonetheless, throughout the production life of this body shell, GM made no effort to make the rear door windows functional.

This was a time of great scrambling and sometimes desperate design moves for Detroit. Ford soldiered on until 1979 with its full-size cars, buffered to some extent by strong sales in its wagon lines. Chrysler, on the other hand, simply abandoned the full-size wagon market completely. The model year 1977 saw the last full-size Chrysler Town and Country, the last Dodge Monaco wagons, and the last full-size Plymouth Suburbans. These three model lines were essentially identical mechanically. In 1976, Chrysler introduced the Plymouth Volare and Dodge Aspen car lines. These cars were only slightly larger than the Valiant and Dart lines, which they were intended to replace. Instead, the Aspen/Volare body shell, which included wagons, became the basis for downsized senior Chrysler products. In 1978, Chrysler introduced a LeBaron Town and Country wagon, which was simply a much-jazzed-up Volare. The Volare/Aspen body later became the basis for the Chrysler Fifth Avenue sedan, which in the 1980s became Chrysler's largest model. Quite a transition for a car introduced as a compact! But it was quite a come-down for Chrysler buyers, to go from a 1977 Town and Country wagon that was 227.7 inches long to a 1978 LeBaron

The sumptuous interior of this custom-built 1975 Cadillac station wagon retained the luxury amenities of the Fleetwood sedan including the folding footrests.

wagon that was only 202.8 inches long. That's a loss of 2 feet in length, which meant something to wagon buyers because it meant a lot less cargo capacity. It was true, the 1978 LeBaron Town and Country had a factory price of $5,848, some $600 less than the 1977 Town and Country factory price of $6,461. The huge reduction in weight, from 4,935 pounds to 3,685 pounds, simply emphasized that from now on car buyers would be getting a lot less car for not much less money. More and more, downsized models came with a higher price tag than their more portly predecessors.

Over at Ford, the response to the challenges of the 1970s moved more slowly. The economical Pinto wagon, especially in four-cylinder form, was definitely in step with the times. A more compact European design-inspired intermediate car line was introduced in the mid-1970s as the Ford Granada and Mercury Monarch. But these cars were not offered as wagons. Meanwhile, the full-size Ford Country Squire carried on in all its wood-trimmed magnificence along with its more plainly trimmed running mates. The intermediate Ford series by the late 1970s was now called LTD II and continued to offer a wagon. But it was a huge car, reaching an astronomical 223 inches in length by 1977, only 2 1/2 inches shorter than the full-size Country Squire. Clearly, such gargantuan cars were increasingly out of step with the surging interest in economy spawned by the energy crisis.

So the intermediate-sized LTD II wagon was dropped for 1978. The full-size Ford LTD and compact Fairmont would have to suffice for wagon buyers. The Pinto was still being produced in 1978, but the end was in sight. For the 1979 model year, Ford finally downsized its big cars. Very much in the Chevrolet Caprice/Impala mold, these cars were boxier and rode on shorter wheelbases with considerably shortened overall length. Yet interior room was actually increased. The sedan version was still known as the LTD,

AMC built a compact wagon on the Hornet platform throughout the 1970s. This 1977 model illustrates the extreme slant of the rear tailgate, which almost made it a hatchback instead of a station wagon. *Byron Olsen Collection*

A 1976 Pontiac Grand LeMans Safari wagon. Although supposedly an intermediate, this wagon was larger than full-size wagons of just a few years earlier. To move this hefty-sized carriage, 400 CID and 455 CID V-8s were available. *Byron Olsen Collection*

This Oldsmobile Cutlass wagon from 1979 shows off the downsized GM intermediate wagon body first introduced in 1978. The same body was offered for several years by Chevrolet, Pontiac, and Buick, but the Olds version was one of the most popular. This Olds was available with everything from V-6 to diesel V-8 engines. *Byron Olsen Collection*

but became the Crown Victoria in 1980. The lineup included a handsome squared-off Country Squire station wagon, still resplendent with imitation woodwork. Mercury also introduced its companion Grand Marquis wagon, which of course used the same body. Thus, as the 1970s ended, Ford had successfully met the downsizing required by the energy crisis. It offered the Pinto wagon, the Fairmont wagon, and the newly downsized LTD Crown Victoria Country Squire station wagon. The name "Crown Victoria" referred to a specialty hardtop model introduced in 1955. The name was attached to the full-sized Ford sedans in 1980, where it has remained to this day.

The new full-size bodies were an excellent design that was popular with the public and stood the test of time and service very well. These cars had almost as long a run as the Chevrolet Caprice, and, like the Caprice, lasted through the 1990 model year.

In 1978, Ford introduced a new line of compact cars called the Fairmont. A wagon was included in the line and so for the first time in years one could once again buy a compact Ford station wagon with four doors. Cargo access was through a one-piece liftgate. This wagon was still rear-wheel drive and offered a choice of four- or six-cylinder engines. Later, a V-8 was also made available. As would be expected from Ford, the top-line Fairmont wagon came with imitation wood side trim. Mercury offered the

same car and called it the Zephyr. These cars were a full 2 1/2 feet shorter than the so-called intermediate LTD II, which they replaced.

American Motors limped through the decade of the 1970s trying to find a market segment in which it could sell in volume. The larger-sized Matador station wagon, whose body design dated back to 1967, was finally discontinued for 1979. Left in its place to serve the wagon market was the compact hatchback introduced in 1971 as the Hornet Sportabout, and the compact Pacer, introduced in station wagon form in 1977. The Pacer was an unusual design on a very short platform but with a large glassy greenhouse. Offered only in two-door form, the wagon version employed a lift-up rear hatch for cargo access. Initially very popular, Pacer sales fell off rapidly by the end of the decade. Although short, the Pacer was not particularly lightweight or economical and it was still very wide. The buying public concluded that it missed the mark as a compact economy car.

The 1970s were not kind to Chrysler Corporation, either. By the end of the decade, the company was in trouble and Lee Iacocca had come galloping to the rescue. After the introduction of the Volare/Aspen twins in 1976, Chrysler began a confusing period of cascading nameplates down to smaller-size body/platform lines. By 1977, the Monaco name, which had previously been reserved for full-size Dodges, was moved down to apply to the intermediate

The 1976 Chrysler Town and Country was one of the largest and most luxurious station wagons on the road. Its days were numbered, as the energy crisis would shortly force the discontinuance of such splendid cruisers as this. Standard equipment included a 440 CID V-8, acres of carpeting, and just about every amenity available on wagons in those days. *Byron Olsen Collection*

series formerly called the Coronet. The big car became the Royal Monaco. As we have already noted, Chrysler soon began expanding the use of the Aspen/Volare design. By 1978, a series of Chryslers was introduced as the LeBaron using the Aspen body and platform. The LeBaron name was formerly reserved for the very top-line Imperials and indeed dated back to the 1930s, when it was a separate company building custom bodies for classic cars.

The LeBaron line included a Town and Country station wagon liberally festooned with bogus woodwork, more so even than the Ford Country Squires. For some reason, the woodwork on these Aspen-based Town and Country wagons did not hold up in service and actually warped, even though it wasn't wood at all but plastic.

This was generally Chrysler's response to the energy crisis: to simply move existing nameplates onto smaller-sized bodies. For 1979, a new full-size New Yorker/Newport body was introduced, but there was no longer a station wagon in the lineup. Only the LeBaron Town and Country wagon brought Chrysler participation in the station wagon market.

Dodge continued to build the Aspen, but made a noticeable effort to reduce the trim level and make the car look plain. The reason was that Dodge had introduced a new line of cars called the Diplomat, but which used the Aspen/Volare body much gussied-up in the manner of the Chrysler LeBaron. Suddenly in 1979, the Coronet intermediate was gone and there was no longer a full-size Dodge station

wagon, either. The Aspen wagon body introduced in 1976 had taken over everything in the station wagon department.

The Aspen/Volare was really an intermediate-size car riding on a 112-inch wheelbase, but with much more reasonable overall length. For example, in 1979, the Aspen wagon was 201 inches long. Its upscale running mate, the Diplomat, was only 1 1/2 inches longer, accounted for by bumper variations. Manufacturers were no longer spending money on different wheelbases

A rear view of the newly downsized GM intermediate wagons, this one a 1978 Pontiac LeMans. The tailgate was unusually wide for the body width and left no room for taillights at the sides. For the first time in years, the rear window lifted up like wagons of the 1950s. Note the lightweight frame and gas-filled struts making the window easy to open. *Byron Olsen Collection*

The GM intermediate body before downsizing, here shown in 1977 Chevrolet Malibu trim. Note the large liftgate and bumper-mounted taillights. *Byron Olsen Collection*

or different sheet metal to differentiate lines of cars. These were stressful times for Detroit and particularly for Chrysler.

Plymouth very much followed the pattern set by Dodge. By 1979, the full-size Plymouth wagon was gone, as was the intermediate Fury. Only Plymouth did not offer an upscale version of the Volare. Thus Plymouth was reduced to a single wagon offering, the Volare.

The Aspen/Volare was a good design for its time, but was initially very poorly executed. Build quality was terrible and service and reliability were equally bad. Over time, Chrysler solved those problems and used this body shell throughout the 1980s. The Aspen/Volare did benefit from the bulletproof super-reliable slant six, which was the engine found in much of the early production. Chrysler small V-8s also had a good reputation. Body corrosion protection was a big problem on these early Aspens and Volares and premature rust-out was a common complaint. But the design was sound and eventually served the Corporation well. By the time it was discontinued in 1988, it was the largest car Chrysler Corporation was building.

All of the design pressures of the 1970s, safety, emissions, and economy, had their effect on station wagon design. More and more smaller-size wagons were introduced while really big full-size wagons became scarce. One of the features of station wagons that made them so appealing to families in the 1950s was the ability to fold the rear seats and turn the entire rear of the car into a mobile playpen for children. But as the 1970s wore on and safety consciousness became stronger, it became evident that this was an unsafe way to travel with children. Today we would not think of allowing kids to float around in the back of a wagon unrestrained. Indeed, it is against the law in many states. This change in the name of safety may have played a part in making wagons less appealing, at least by the 1990s.

All of these winds of change battered the automobile industry so that the cars offered in 1980 looked far different than they had in 1970. There were fewer wagons to choose from and those that were for sale were generally smaller in size and less powerful. Yet wagons continued to make up nearly 10 percent of total industry production into the early years of the 1980s. But the 1980s were to bring a stunning change in the wagon market in the form of the minivan.

One of the few new wagon designs of the 1990s, a 1995 Mercury Sable. A near twin of its corporate sibling the Ford Taurus, the Sable was the largest passenger car–based station wagon built in the United States at the end of the 1990s.

CHAPTER 7

The 1980s and 1990s

THE STATION WAGON FADES AWAY

If the 1970s were a decade of difficult transition for automobile manufacturers, the 1980s were no better. The combined pressure of the need for improved energy efficiency, reduced air pollution, compact size, and more safety left the industry in disarray and confusion. As the manufacturers scrambled to meet these new requirements, there remained an overriding fear that, once all these objectives were met, the public might not like what they were offered. This happened on occasion in the 1980s, particularly to General Motors, which went too far in downsizing in the mid-1980s.

Downsizing posed a particular threat to station wagons. After all, people bought station wagons so they could haul around lots of people and stuff. If you make the wagon smaller, will it have the same appeal?

The energies of the manufacturers were greatly sapped by the need to meet all of the safety, emission, and fuel-efficiency requirements being mandated by the federal government. In fairness, this was not just something being handed down by a dictatorial government: the people of the United States on the whole supported efforts to reduce the impact of automobiles on American society, which was already overwhelming. Air quality and congestion in major urban centers such as Los Angeles were clearly the result of too many automobiles producing too much exhaust emissions.

Because the financial and human resources of automobile companies were stretched by these demands, the body cycle change rate slowed down dramatically. In the 1950s, a complete new body shell was brought out every three years for each marque and sometimes even more frequently. But

by the late 1960s, that pace had slowed considerably. Part of the problem was that, after 1960, each manufacturer was now marketing not one but several different sizes of cars, each requiring its own platform or body shell. Senior General Motors cars, for example, used one body shell from 1965 through the 1970 model year: six years in total. During a cycle, a body shell would have the exterior sheet metal changed from time to time to distinguish one GM brand from another, and to distinguish the model year. But the inner structure would remain basically unchanged through the cycle. This trend continued in the 1980s and the body cycle times stretched even more.

Wagon sales in the 1980s flattened out and then began to decline. The trend accelerated dramatically in the 1990s until now, and as the millennium approaches, there are very few U.S.-built automobile-based station wagons left on the market. For the 1999 model year, Ford offered but two wagon bodies, a few import manufacturers offered a wagon here or there, General Motors offered only little Saturns, and Chrysler offered no station wagons at all. What in the world had happened? Why had America's preferred family car of the 1960s disappeared?

Several things occurred to bring about this change. First, cars got smaller, making the station wagon a less attractive alternative for people who really needed to haul a lot of stuff around. They looked for a bigger vehicle, such as a pickup or a van. Second and most decisive was the arrival of the modern minivan in 1984. Introduced by Chrysler Corporation, these new minivans were front-wheel drive and thus had a relatively low floor and low overall height. They drove and handled more like a passenger car than previous vans large or small. The new breed of minivan was designed from the outset as a car. Earlier small vans from the 1960s were usually scaled-down trucks.

The new minivans were economical, well trimmed and equipped, and most important held a lot more than the average station wagon. The interiors were higher and the cargo length was comparable to a station wagon. Yet outside, the overall length was considerably shorter than even an intermediate-size station wagon of the 1970s. The Chrysler-designed minivan was really a modern miracle in that the buyer got more space and more passenger capacity for less money and less fuel consumption. And sacrificed nothing in comfort or luxury or easy handling.

A third trend that had been growing for some time was the popularity of pickup trucks. We think of the truck and sport utility vehicle (SUV) revolution as a recent phenomenon, but for more than two decades the largest-selling passenger vehicle in America has often been the Ford F150 pickup truck. By that we mean a vehicle bought primarily for passenger travel rather than specifically to haul something. This trend has accelerated dramatically in the 1990s.

Finally, the slow steady growth of the SUV market led by the Jeep Wagoneer and Jeep Cherokee caught fire and became an avalanche. By the end of the 1990s, every manufacturer, domestic and imported alike, was offering a four-wheel-drive sport utility vehicle, usually truck-based. It doesn't take a genius to tell at a glance that all SUVs are really station wagon bodies mounted up on four-wheel drive truck chassis with bigger tires and higher road clearance.

So the station wagon hasn't really gone away. Instead, it has been transformed into a more commodious family vehicle in the form of the minivan or in the form of the SUV, a go-anywhere vehicle with less emphasis on cargo capacity than upon mobility off road.

These shifts were evident by the end of the 1980s. In 1983, on the eve of the introduction of the Chrysler minivans, stations wagons still commanded 10 percent of the industry market share. Five short years after the minivan was introduced, the station wagon market share had dropped to under 5 percent. Clearly, a dramatic shift was under way and it wasn't too difficult to figure out the cause.

The individual manufacturers reacted to the shifting trends in a number of ways.

The cargo area of the 1995 Mercury Sable. There is less room here than in wagons of the past, although this car is equipped with a rudimentary third seat. By the 1990s, Detroit was assuming that if you wanted to haul cargo, you bought a minivan or a pickup.

Chrysler, the inventor of the modern front-drive minivan, soon placed all of its faith in the minivan as the answer for those who needed wagons. All of Chrysler Corporation's large and so-called intermediate-size wagons were blown away by 1979, victims of a combination of the energy crisis, dropping sales, and corporate financial problems.

In 1976, Chrysler introduced the Plymouth Volare and the Dodge Aspen, two identical cars that came in four-door, coupe, and station wagon form. This was to be the new replacement for both the mid-size cars as well as the compact Valiant and Dart. Very quickly, by 1978, Chrysler took the Volare/Aspen wagon body and began offering it with a

The 1985 Dodge Aries K. The square design produced a roomy wagon on a small platform. This was Chrysler Corporation's last conventional station wagon design and was also offered in Plymouth Reliant and Chrysler Town and Country trim. Power came from a front-wheel-drive 2.2-liter four-cylinder engine. The last year of production for these last Chrysler wagons was 1988. *Byron Olsen Collection*

A Chevrolet Cavalier CS wagon from 1987. The J-body GM compact car introduced in 1982 was another GM front-drive response to the downsizing era that drew only mediocre reviews. Nevertheless, this platform remained in production for more than a decade and at one time was being sold under all GM nameplates. *Byron Olsen Collection*

A case study in downsizing by shifting nameplates. The wood-trimmed wagon is a 1978 Ford Fairmont Squire, its first year. The Fairmont was introduced as a compact, fuel-efficient car to meet the energy crisis. By 1984, the same car was being sold as a top-of-the-line intermediate LTD model. Body sheet metal was unchanged, the wheelbase remained 105.5 inches, while weight and overall length increased only fractionally. But by virtue of the more prestigious place in the Ford lineup, price had more than doubled, going from $4,151 to $9,102! *Byron Olsen Collection*

Chrysler nameplate as the LeBaron. This was a more upscale version and was joined by a fancier Dodge version called the Diplomat. Through 1980, all four of these wagons were marketed, and were all essentially identical underneath the exterior trim variations. Wheelbase was the same 112.7 inches, engines were the same, and length varied no more than 1 inch. By 1981, the Volare and Aspen were discontinued and by 1982 the LeBaron and Diplomat were dumped as well.

This was a time of trial for Chrysler Corporation: Lee Iacocca had come to the rescue from his previous position as head of Ford. The car lines, especially the larger cars, were slashed mercilessly and replaced in 1981 with the K-cars. These were much shorter, squared-off cars with front-wheel drive and four-cylinder engines. The Plymouth version was named Reliant, the Dodge version Aries, and the Chrysler variation LeBaron. They were offered as four-door and two-door sedans, station wagons, and even a convertible for a time. After 1981, the K-cars were the only station wagons offered by Chrysler Corporation. The K-car platform was offered in an ever-widening variety of body styles and trim levels, and was Chrysler's mainstay product throughout the decade of the 1980s. Truly it was the car that saved the company: that, and the minivan arriving in the middle of the decade. At first a low-priced compact car sold with Plymouth and Dodge labels, the K-car eventually was marketed in a longer wheelbase and much-gussied-up version as a Chrysler New Yorker. The early Dodge Aries/Plymouth Reliants had a 100-inch wheelbase and were only 176 inches long. Yet because front-wheel drive eliminated

drivetrain intrusion into the passenger compartment, and because the styling was very boxy, the cars had a surprising amount of room inside. All versions of the K-car station wagon went out of production after 1988.

The minivan arrived in 1984 and was first sold as a Dodge Caravan and in nearly identical form as the Plymouth Voyager. It was an overnight runaway success that has hardly abated as of the end of the 1990s. General Motors and Ford were reluctant to admit that Chrysler had come up with a winner and stubbornly resisted adopting the front-drive, relatively low-height, easy-handling format so successfully pioneered by Chrysler. Instead, both Ford and Chevrolet first brought out what were essentially scaled-down trucklike big vans. The Ford Aerostar and Chevrolet Astro both had rear-wheel drive, which meant the floor had to be noticeably higher off the ground to clear the driveline. This, in turn, meant the whole vehicle had to be higher than a Chrysler minivan to get the same amount of room inside. Neither made as good use of interior space as the Chrysler minivans and neither sold nearly as well. The Dodge Caravan and Plymouth Voyager mopped up the field. They were joined in 1990 by a Chrysler Town and Country version, which replaced the last K-car station wagons.

The Ford Aerostar and Chevrolet Astro/GMC Safari eventually found a market niche as all-wheel-drive vehicles. They were hefty enough to pull trailers in that configuration, something a front-drive van could not do as well.

Chrysler Corporation did have another wagon up its sleeve by the end of the 1980s. It

had acquired American Motors in 1987 and with it the Jeep franchise and product line. The compact-size Jeep Cherokee station wagon was already a big success when Chrysler took over AMC. The Grand Wagoneer, introduced in 1963 by Kaiser/Jeep, continued to sell well for close to three decades. It was not taken out of production until 1991. The Grand Wagoneer was also a station wagon body design and was built in both two-door and four-door formats. As we have seen, this was the car that really started the sport utility craze. The Wagoneer had many traditional station wagon design characteristics. Most sold had four doors, the rear seat folded quickly to create more cargo space, and the rear tailgate employed a crank-down window that rolled down into the tailgate. Like most SUVs since, it was available with two-wheel or four-wheel drive, but most were sold with four-wheel drive. That feature, after all, was what had made Jeep famous in the first place.

General Motors and Ford were slower to abandon the station wagon. Partly because they were larger companies and had more internal policy-making inertia, and partly because their minivans were not as successful as the Chrysler versions, both Ford and GM continued to offer wagons well into the 1990s.

The first downsized GM intermediate body shell was introduced in 1978, and included a station wagon in the lineup. It was still rear-wheel drive and was sold in wagon form by four GM divisions through 1983. The reader will recall that this is the body design that reverted to a traditional lift-up transom and a drop-down tailgate and did not offer the option of a doorgate. Chevrolet's version was the Malibu, Pontiac's the LeMans Safari, Oldsmobile's the Cutlass Cruiser, and Buick's the Century Estate.

By 1983, when these rear-drive GM intermediates were on their last legs, GM brought out a whole new line of front-wheel-drive intermediate-size cars. Chevrolet's version was called the Celebrity, Pontiac's the 6000, Oldsmobile the Ciera, and Buick again turned to the Century nameplate. Sedan versions

The 1998 Saturn S-series station wagon, almost the last new car-based wagon introduced by any General Motors division in the twentieth century. The short rear end of the S-series shows that cargo capacity was not a major design criterion. Saturn also introduced a new, larger-size wagon in 1999 in the L-series. By this time, it was the only GM division to offer station wagons.

117

Ford's benchmark Country Squire seen here near the end of its long reign as America's most successful big station wagon. Introduced in 1979, the body design shown here was produced virtually unchanged for a remarkable 11 years before disappearing forever after 1990. This is a 1987 LTD version and still carries the trademark Country Squire wood side trim. *Byron Olsen Collection*

arrived in 1982, but the wagon versions did not come out until 1984 to replace the previous generation of intermediate wagons that went out of production at the same time.

These were pleasant although unexciting cars and were GM's first major front-wheel-drive wagon entrants in the intermediate-size class. But these cars sold well, and in Oldsmobile and Buick form, were marketed for a remarkable 13 model years. They didn't go out of production until 1995. Some felt they should have been retired years before because, by that time, they were no longer state-of-the-art in many ways.

These cars were built on what GM referred to as the A-body platform. They were good practical cars and were usually sold with one of GM's ubiquitous V-6 pushrod engines originally developed by Buick in 1961. They served well but excited very few people. By the time the Buick Century and Oldsmobile Ciera finally went out of production in the mid-1990s, they were an all-too-visible reminder that GM had lost its competitive edge. Chevrolet and Pontiac had dropped use of this platform by 1990 and 1991, respectively.

Another uninspiring GM car, but a long-running one, nevertheless, was the J car platform

introduced in 1982 as the Chevrolet Cavalier and Pontiac Sunbird. This was a very compact front-wheel-drive GM platform and was also criticized by the motoring press for lack of innovation. Joined for a time by Oldsmobile and Buick versions including wagons (the Firenza and Sky-hawk) the platform was in production for more than a decade. There was even a Cadillac version called the Cimarron, which did nothing to enhance Cadillac's prestige. The Cimarron was not offered as a wagon. At a time when the competition was heating up with mushrooming sales of imported cars with better reliability and more complete equipment, these two platforms were a poor way for General Motors to position itself for the competitive battles of the 1990s.

Surprisingly, the most successful station wagon story at GM in the 1980s were the full-size wagons introduced in 1977 as the first downsized versions of GM's big cars. These big wagons were sold in nearly identical form by four General Motors divisions. Led by the Chevrolet Impala and Caprice, the Oldsmobile Custom Cruiser, and the Buick LeSabre and Electra Estate wagons, and joined from time to time by Pontiac versions sometimes labeled Bonneville or Parisienne, these wagons had a remarkably long run. They lasted until the 1990 model year, an incredible 14-year span. In their last year of production, they still bore a remarkable resemblance to the first-year car even to the size and type of engine most commonly used: A five-liter V-8. Even after the senior Oldsmobiles and Buicks were downsized and made front-wheel drives in 1985 (with disastrous sales results), these two GM divisions continued to market the big rear-drive wagons without change. They recognized that wagon buyers wanted capacity and apparently felt that the new downsized Buick LeSabres and Oldsmobile Eighty-Eights and Ninety-Eights simply could not offer enough room to be appealing in wagon form. No wagons were ever offered on these new downsized front-wheel-drive GM senior cars.

When the string ran out on this remarkable 14-year run, many observers assumed that GM would abandon the large rear-drive wagon field. But GM's downsized front-wheel-drive "big" cars, which weren't very big, were selling poorly. Meanwhile, Ford was continuing to

have good sales success with its big cars, the Ford Crown Victoria, Mercury Grand Marquis, and the Lincoln Town Car. Ford and Mercury continued to offer large wagons through the 1990 model year.

So in an effort to recapture a piece of the large car market, which GM had lamely abandoned, a new full-sized rear-wheel-drive platform was designed and introduced for the 1991 model year. The only rear-wheel-drive GM sedans still in production up to that time had been the Chevrolet Caprice/Impala and Cadillac Fleetwood Brougham. The Chevrolet was largely being sold for fleet use as taxis and police cars. The new body was large, very rounded, and aerodynamic in the style of the time, and represented a radical departure from its predecessor. The new body had an extremely slanted windshield and rear window in the Chevrolet version. The Buick and Cadillac sedan versions squared off the rear of the greenhouse in a more traditional fashion. The beltline was widened out to the full width of the car and the side glass curved significantly

A 1987 Escort, Ford's compact replacement for the Pinto at the compact-size end of the line-up. The Escort was designed and sold as a world car. Ford continued to offer an Escort station wagon throughout the 1990s. There is some question whether all of those large model sailboats will fit in the back of this compact wagon. *Byron Olsen Collection*

The 1993 Buick Roadmaster Estate Wagon. This was America's last grand station wagon and was built from 1991 through 1996. The Buick Estate Wagon carried its faux woodwork to the bitter end. The rounded aerodynamic styling made the car look even larger than it was.

in from the extreme width of the car at the beltline to the top of the doors. The intention was to make the car rounded and aerodynamic. But the unfortunate result was that it simply looked fat and ungainly, particularly in the rear wheel/C-pillar area. The Buick and Cadillac sedans looked a bit slimmer than the Chevrolet Caprice version, because of the more squared-off rear window area of the two larger cars.

An even bigger surprise was that GM designed a wagon body for this new large-size platform. It was a fitting last hurrah for what was to be GM's last new full-size car-based station wagon body design. It was initially sold in Chevrolet, Oldsmobile, and Buick versions, but Oldsmobile marketed theirs for only two years, 1991 and 1992. The Chevrolet and Buick versions lasted until 1996, when the entire platform was taken out of production to provide more plant capacity to produce trucks and SUVs.

But the real reason it went out of production was that it had bombed in the marketplace. It just looked too fat. Styling tweaks on the Chevrolet Caprice during its production life enlarged the rear wheel openings, changed

Another view of the last Buick Estate Wagon. The unique glass skylight over the rear seat is just visible. Also evident is the glass tailgate and rotund styling.

Another version of GM's ubiquitous J-body cars, this one appearing as a 1986 Oldsmobile Firenza Cruiser. During the mid-1980s, you could buy this same wagon with four different nameplates, which shared both exterior sheet metal and mechanical components. This Olds version is classed-up with imitation wood applique, wire wheel covers, and a roof rack. *Byron Olsen Collection*

the angle of the rear quarter windows and reduced the ponderous fat look of the rear of the car. An Impala SS version was brought out that was aggressive and much better-looking with blacked-out chrome and huge wheels. But it didn't help enough. The public stayed away in droves and bought Ford Crown Victorias. Part of the reason the car was not terribly successful is that, although it was a large body on the outside, the exterior size didn't translate into a particularly roomy back seat. The windshield and side window glass were farther from the occupants than many were used to and it made some people uncomfortable.

As a last hurrah for big General Motors' station wagons, these cars did offer some interesting features. The Oldsmobile and Buick versions brought back the skylight glass panel over the rear seat, much like the Vista-Cruiser marketed in the mid-1960s. This time around it was referred to as the Vista roof. The Chevrolet version did not have the glass roof panel. The Vista roof versions did not have the extra panels of glass in the roof sides over the cargo area that were found in the old Vista-Cruisers. The third seat in these wagons, when that option was chosen, was a rear-facing version, unlike the Vista-Cruisers of the 1960s.

These wagons came with a built-in roof rack. The tailgate arrangement was unusual. The doorgate returned, but instead of rolling down into the gate, the rear window flipped up in transom fashion as in the 1950s. Now, however, the transom was a sheet of tempered glass without any framing at all. It was light and easy to flip open and was held up by gas-filled struts.

Also standard equipment was a rear window washer-wiper mounted at the top of the liftgate. The Buick versions of these wagons usually came lavishly equipped with leather seating. There were storage compartments and cubbyholes all over the rear cargo area. Third seats were practically standard equipment and all three wagons provided operating vent windows in the rear side glass for third-seat passengers.

Oldsmobile continued to call its version the Custom Cruiser and Chevrolet offered its version as a Caprice. Buick resurrected a name from its past and called its version the Roadmaster Estate Wagon. All three cars had the same 116-inch wheelbase and all three were within a half-inch of each other in overall length, a whopping 217 inches plus.

Engines were much the same in all three as well. The Chevrolet and Oldsmobile could be had with a 5-liter 305 CID engine as standard and a 5.7-liter (350 CID) V-8 as an option. The Roadmaster came only with the 5.7-liter engine and later in the production run, used the Corvette LT l block!

As noted earlier, none of these cars sold well. Oldsmobile offered only the wagon and did not sell a sedan version of the big Caprice body. The Custom Cruiser wagon was dropped after only two years. The Buick and Chevrolet wagon versions, however, soldiered on to the end of the production run of these bodies in the 1996 model year. It can be said that General Motors ended the large station wagon era with a good deal of style and majesty. Whatever one thinks of the aesthetic beauty of these cars, they were large, lavishly equipped, and traditional station wagons through and through. And the Chevrolet and Buick versions even offered imitation woodwork on the flanks right up to the bitter end. Some ideas just die hard.

In retrospect, tooling up for a big new station wagon in the 1990s was a mistake. The market just wasn't there anymore. Sometimes one can't be sure a market is gone until one tries to sell something in it and nobody buys. One reason GM offered these big wagons was because of the booming popularity of camping trailers and other recreational vehicles. More and more people had hefty trailers to tow and the shrinking size of most popular cars and front-wheel drive just did not lend themselves to serious towing. As it turned out, however, people with serious towing to do were buying even more serious towing vehicles: the Chevrolet and GMC Suburbans and big pickup trucks. All of the truck-based vehicles had become smoother-riding, easier to handle, and now boasted luxurious interiors. It was no longer a sacrifice or hardship to have to ride in a truck all day: they were just as comfortable as a sedan or a station wagon.

Enter the villain, the car that shot the station wagon. This is the first modern minivan, the 1984 Dodge Caravan, the car and the concept that revolutionized the wagon market. The woodwork on the side and the luggage rack on the roof are about the only reminders of the station wagon heritage. *Byron Olsen Collection*

These grand wagons were nevertheless not the last General Motors station wagons built on a passenger car platform. A new nameplate quietly appeared in the General Motors lineup in 1991. The compact Saturn was created from scratch as not only a whole new car, but a whole new way of building and marketing automobiles. The Saturn was not developed by any existing General Motors division, nor was it built by any existing General Motors plants. It was an effort by GM to create a new car design and marketing culture and reach the segment of the marketplace taken over by compact, economical Japanese imports such as Toyota Corolla and Honda Civic. Some people at GM realized that if the Corporation was going to break new ground, it would have to do it in an environment far removed from Detroit.

Although costly, the effort appears to have succeeded. The Saturn has become reasonably popular and is marketed through independent dealerships on a no-haggle, no-hassle basis. Saturns appear to be bought largely by people who are not car enthusiasts and just want an automobile that's reliable and dealers who are pleasant.

Introduced in four-door sedan and coupe form, in 1993 Saturn added a station wagon. It was, of course, very small, with a 102-inch wheelbase and 1.9-liter four-cylinder engine. The rear seat offered a split-fold arrangement and the tailgate was a one-piece liftgate. The rear-wheel suspension towers intruded rather significantly into the cargo area, but clearly no one was buying a wagon this small for high cubic capacity. Curb weight was around 2,400 pounds and overall length was an easy-to-park 176 inches.

For 1996, the Saturn four-door sedan and station wagon were completely redesigned. Thus, as the big Caprice and Roadmaster station wagons were being taken out of production, GM introduced its last new car-based station wagon, the diminutive Saturn. Actually, not quite the last. In 1999, Saturn introduced another new wagon in the new L-series line. This is a larger car meant to complement the smaller S-series, which remains in production. Only time will tell whether Saturns will really build the last GM wagons. For 1999, Saturn was the only GM division to offer station wagons.

Of course, it is misleading and simply incorrect to think that General Motors has abandoned the large station wagon market. Today one of GM's most popular line of vehicles is the Chevy/GMC Suburban and Tahoe/Yukon. The Suburban is a consistent evolution of the original all-steel Chevy Suburban introduced in 1935. There are now four side doors instead of two but otherwise the concept remains the same: a truck-based, three-seat, all-steel station wagon-type vehicle with windows all around.

The current Chevy Tahoe and GMC Yukon are slightly shortened versions of the big Suburban. The Tahoe/Yukon at just under 200 inches overall length are 20 inches shorter than the big Suburban. The Suburban wheelbase is 131.5 inches, compared to 117.5 inches for the shorter version. Both vehicles have independent front suspension and approach passenger car riding comfort. They offer a huge array of options, including four-wheel drive, and engine choices ranging up to 7.4 liters or a 6.5-liter diesel V-8. These vehicles

have more cargo room than traditional car-based station wagons and, when properly equipped, can haul bigger trailers than any traditional station wagon ever could. For GM, the station wagon market hasn't gone away, it has just changed. GM is still working to meet the challenge.

General Motors' wagons and small vans offer a couple of interesting alternative ways to access the cargo area. The Suburban/Tahoe/Yukon offer a choice of drop-down tailgates and lift-up transoms, or as an alternative, two-panel truck-type side-hinged doors. This has been a long-standing choice on these vehicles. The Chevy Astro/GMC Safari minivan, which was originally introduced as a rear-wheel-drive, short-wheelbase competitor to the Chrysler minivans, has now evolved into a longer wheelbase, all-wheel-drive trailer hauler. The Astro/Safari offers an optional rear opening that is a combination of doors and liftgate. The upper panel, or transom, lifts up in traditional station wagon form. But the lower gate is split and hinged at the sides, and opens as two Dutch doors.

The most common cargo access method on today's remaining wagons and many SUVs is a one-piece liftgate with the added convenience of being able to open the window panel separately to reach in and remove small objects.

The minivan that conquered the station wagon. This is a 1992 Plymouth Voyager, the third facelift of the original Chrysler minivan from 1984. This is the short-wheelbase model and shows the characteristic sliding side door and large one-piece rear liftgate. These remarkable minivans had room for much bulkier objects within a package that was dramatically shorter in overall length compared to a conventional station wagon.

The entire liftgate to which the window is hinged lifts up for more wide open access.

Another wagon innovation now widely available on wagon-type bodies is a privacy panel for the cargo area. A window shadelike screen can be pulled rearward from its storage position by the second seat backrest to conceal small items in the cargo bay. The idea is to discourage thievery by concealing attractive objects that might invite a break-in.

The Taurus and Escort were not Ford's only entries into the station wagon market of the 1990s. After decades of watching sales of General Motors' Suburbans growing, Ford finally introduced the Expedition in 1997 based on the newly redesigned F150 full-size pickup truck chassis. Ford was already leading the SUV market with the midsize Explorer and its Mercury twin, the Mountaineer. The Expedition was a few inches longer in wheelbase and length than a Chevy Tahoe, but considerably shorter than a Suburban. And as the millennium approached, Ford introduced its biggest station wagon yet, a huge Suburban-type vehicle called the Excursion based on the Ford F350 heavy-duty pickup chassis. The Navigator, Lincoln's version of the Expedition, has been the hottest thing going in the luxury car market since its introduction.

In the late 1990s, Ford Motor Company was the only major manufacturer continuing to offer a choice of traditional car-based station wagons. Through the 1980s, the big Ford Country Squire and Mercury Grand Marquis wagons introduced in 1979 had almost as long a production run as the 1977 Chevrolet Caprice. The big Ford wagons lasted through the 1990 model year. Unlike GM, however, when Ford redesigned its full-size rear-drive car in 1991, it did not produce a station wagon version. The Ford Crown Victoria looked much sleeker than the Chevrolet Caprice and was definitely trimmer in the waistline. It sold well throughout the 1990s, and by the end of the decade had completely replaced Chevrolet in the taxi and police car fleets of the nations. This is another example of General Motors abandoning a market segment that it had long dominated.

By the end of their long model run in 1990, the last Ford Country Squire and the Mercury Marquis station wagons were being promoted for their trailer-hauling ability and abundant floor space. An automatic load-leveling option was available to compensate for heavy loads or heavy trailers. Eight people could be carried with optional side-facing rear seats.

Trailer-towing equipment included higher-ratio rear axle, limited-slip differentials, heavy-duty cooling system and suspensions, and dual exhaust. Like the GM large wagons, the standard engine was a 5.0-liter V-8. Interiors could be lavishly turned out in genuine leather with center armrest and split front seats. Ford's traditional doorgate provided the access to the cargo area. There was one more Ford tradition that was continued to the end of these big haulers: imitation woodwork on the exterior. Faithful to established tradition, woodgrained sides were outlined by wood-appearing strips on the Ford while the Mercury woodgrain was edged with bright metal strips.

With the retirement of the Country Squire in 1990, Ford was not out of the wagon business entirely, however. In 1986, Ford introduced the first Taurus and its Mercury clone, the Sable. These cars broke dramatically with Ford styling practice and were very round and aerodynamic. They were immediately popular and sold well for 10 years until their replacements were introduced for the 1996 model year.

Both Taurus and Sable offered a station wagon model with familiar features: folding rear seats and a liftgate in the back. The aerodynamic lines did not make for a huge cargo area, but like all wagons, the folding seat offered flexible utilization of the interior space. These cars were intermediate in size and became Ford's best-selling car line. In some years, the Taurus has been the best-selling passenger car in the U.S. market.

In 1996, an entirely new Taurus and Sable were introduced. These cars were even more aerodynamic than the first, but were not as well received. Ford went overboard with making everything oval shaped: the windows, especially the rear cargo area windows on the wagon, and even the heater and radio control panel. The wagon version is still offered as of 1999 and it now stands alone as the only medium-size American-built station wagon.

In the compact Ford Escort and Mercury Lynx lines, Ford also continued to offer station wagons through the 1990s. All in all, this represented quite a dramatic shrinkage of a once major segment of the American automobile market. But it would not be accurate to conclude that the station wagon is dead and gone. Several imports with significant U.S. market share continue to offer traditional station wagons. Such makes as Volvo and Subaru continue to sell a good many station wagons in both the compact and intermediate-size ranges. Some offer all-wheel-drive versions, geared not so much for off-road use, but better traction generally. Volkswagen, Audi, BMW, and Mercedes Benz also offer station wagons. The traditional wagon hasn't disappeared, but the choice has become more limited.

The basic concept that made the station wagon body style so popular is definitely alive and well. By that we mean a vehicle with all of the floor space back of the dashboard available alternatively for passenger or cargo use by means of folding or removable passenger seats and a squared-off body in the rear. After all, this is the design principle governing the minivan and it is also the design principle that governs most sport utility vehicles. These vehicles all have cargo area in the rear accessible from the passenger area and they all have some form of tailgate or liftgate in the back to load large objects. The minivan emphasizes greater cargo and interior space, while the typical SUV emphasizes off-road capability through hefty running gear and correspondingly less emphasis on a big interior. But the principle is the same for all of these vehicles. All offer greater flexibility and greater utilization of the interior space. And that's the most significant contribution the station wagon has made to automotive design.

Index